In memoriam
Mary Rose Goodwin (née Didd)
(1934–2008)
Wesley John Goodwin (1932–2009)

To
Tamara, Saskia, and Mum … love and
thanks for many different reasons.

Contents

List of figures and tables

Figures

Table

Acknowledgements

I would like to express my sincere thanks to all those that have contributed to the development of the ideas explored in this book, namely Professor Corinne May-Chahal, Professor Karen Broadhurst, Dr Paula Doherty and Dr Emma Vickers, and to all the professionals for the valuable contributions that formed the foundations of this book; without their time, patience, honesty and willingness to talk about, and debate, the issues raised, this book would never have happened. I would also like to thank Paul Thompson, my family and friends, and treasured colleagues at the University of Bedfordshire who have offered invaluable advice and support over many years. Last, but by no means least, I would like to extend my sincere gratitude to Professor Sue White not only for taking the time to read this book and write the foreword, but also for the consistent support she has given me in my role as an early career academic.

Foreword

This book addresses a recurrent theme in the reporting of, and responses to, child protection tragedies in the UK and internationally. When systems fail and professional judgements retrospectively prove to be wrong, shrill exhortations for professionals to share information to facilitate better multi-agency working are once again recharged and the volume cranked up. This book provides a welcome analysis of why 'information sharing' remains a wicked issue.

Research, including my own, shows that knowledge sharing and learning are influenced by multiple interpersonal, social and organisational factors. The identification of children at risk and the sharing of knowledge and decision making across time and space may properly be conceived as a complex system, whereby inter-dependencies and couplings between professionals and agencies can be both the source of safety but also a risk, depending on how they are 'done'. The promotion of multi-agency working with children and families is promoted as a way to prevent children 'slipping through the net' of services, and of ensuring that professionals have the 'full picture'. The literature repeatedly emphasises that good communication has the potential to reduce this complexity and support coordination, but what does communication mean and how does one know when it has taken place?

Knowledge sharing is more than the transmission of information. It denotes the exchange and use of diverse knowledge, and often more tacit 'know-how', between different groups to engender shared understanding. But, as this book shows, knowledge is difficult to share and it typically acquired and developed through participation in 'communities of practice', rather than management information systems. In short, knowledge is not a 'thing' that a community 'has', but rather it is what they 'do', 'make' and who they 'are'. This distinction is important because efforts to understand, and indeed promote knowledge sharing and collaboration, should focus not only on the formal assemblages of knowledge, but also the more informal and unarticulated manifestations of know-how. Recognising these differences, knowledge sharing requires different strategies and practices. The sharing of tacit knowledge is often based on more informal, day-to-day interactions around common problems, the creation of opportunities to enable social intercourse and creative problem solving. The detailed empirical work in this book shows how professional sense making is constrained by the local organisational practices that disrupt relationships and reduce or eliminate proximity.

Child welfare services are caught in a perpetual tension between the rights of the many to help and freedom from unwelcome scrutiny and intrusive intervention into the intimate spaces of family life and those of the relatively few who come to serious harm. The precautionary principle is constantly in a dance with proportionality. The policy response to high-profile events has been to standardise processes and seek 'consistent thresholds'. This, it has been argued, would ensure safety in the system. In fact, it has led to a great deal of 'screening' behaviour and short-term, multiple assessments in children's services often at the expense of practical help and sustained relational support. Services become increasingly distanced from families, communities and from each other. Technology is held up as the solution to this distance – it can facilitate efficient information sharing and timely responses across time and space.

This book shows us why this is not so simple. For example, attempts to manage risk in the multi-agency system and encourage a 'referring culture' can have the unintended consequence of swamping children's social care. This leads to gatekeeping practices to manage demand, which in turn can spawn precipitous reorganisation and instability. Meanwhile, other agencies feel they are left holding unacceptable levels of risk and thus they are compelled to refer. Professionals and their managers have been caught in a sea of contradictory imperatives and attempts to manage complexity have too often led to complicated structures, systems and sign-offs and an attempt to slice practice into simple chunks.

In this book, Kellie Thompson rightly problematises the 'jigsaw' metaphor. I agree that it is misleading. Who knows what the full picture is, and whether some of the pieces are missing? An approach to knowledge sharing that attends properly to human factors would be more like a web, where professionals remain connected to each other and to the knowledge they are sharing. Reading this book will help policymakers and managers to design their services with communication in mind and will ensure that practitioners are aware of each other's (mis)interpretive practices. It is a must-read antidote to simplistic policy mantras.

Sue White
Professor of Social Work (Children and Families)
University of Birmingham

ONE

Introduction

If we are together nothing is impossible. If we are divided all will fail. (Winston Churchill, Honorary degree acceptance speech at Harvard University, 6 September 1943, cited in Gilbert, 2005, p 283)

On 11 November 1918, when the guns of the Western Front finally fell silent, Winston Churchill (the then Minister of Munitions) reflected retrospectively on the war that had just ended (Gilbert, 2005). He concluded that if America had joined forces with the Allies much earlier in the conflict, Germany could have been defeated much sooner, and importantly, the fatalities that occurred during the First World War could have been prevented (Gilbert, 2005). With the advent of the Second World War, Churchill drew on his experiences during the First World War to call for unity in the Second: unity among the allies, and unity among the people of Britain. In the context of war, declarations such as Churchill's may be seen as morally rhetorical, that is, pervasive devices used during an emotionally charged time of uncertainty, fear and death – who could refute Churchill's claim that 'working together' to defeat the enemy was not a good idea given the threat posed to the stability and security of the nation at that time?

In a child welfare context, political messages from high-profile public inquiries following the deaths of children resonate with Churchill's call for unity, and more specifically with the retrospective notion that tragic child abuse fatalities could have been prevented if professionals had worked together, communicated and shared relevant information more effectively. Similar to lives that have been regrettably lost in war, the deaths of children provide a powerful emotive context for the delivery and acceptance of key messages and mantras. For example, the appellation 'every child matters' in 2003 was fostered following the widely media publicised death of an eight-year-old West African child, Victoria Climbié, who – on 25 February 2000 – was killed by her great-aunt Marie-Thérèse Kouao, and Kouao's partner Carl John Manning, through severe cruelty and neglect. The tragic circumstances that surrounded Victoria's death created a public and professional climate keen to receive recommendations regarding prevention. Reiterating the sentiment posed by Churchill, who could possibly reject the idea that professionals should work together effectively to prevent children from harm? On the basis of messages from high-profile child death inquiries, this question has given rise to a number of 'quality improvement' projects to 'fix' recurrent issues in multi-agency working and information sharing.

Working together across multi-agency settings to improve information sharing has now become a moral and political imperative in England and Wales for improving the welfare and the protection of children. Following a spate of highly publicised child deaths, including those of seven-year-old Maria Colwell in 1973 (Colwell Report, 1974), Victoria Climbié in 2000, 17-month-old Peter Connelly in 2007 (Haringey LSCB, 2008) and, more recently, four-year-old Daniel Pelka in 2012 (Coventry LSCB, 2013) serious case reviews (SCRs) have frequently raised concerns regarding the ability of professionals to work together and share information effectively. Indeed, failings in multi-agency 'communication' and 'information sharing' have haunted professional child welfare practices for over four decades. Nevertheless, despite 'information sharing' being a ubiquitous feature of SCRs, this aspect of institutional practice remains poorly understood. In other words, we still are not any closer in wholly resolving the issues consistently identified in such reports. This has been reflected in the dominant response to past failings, which have been considered in very narrow, 'rational-bureaucratic' terms (Ferguson, 2007, p 781) while not getting much closer to solving the problem. Under the administration of the Conservative government, and the Prime Minister

David Cameron's calls for even greater austerity measures, little has changed. Imposed pressures of performance management targets fuelled by Ofsted inspections, funding cuts and calls for local authorities to make efficiency savings have meant changes in the way cases are managed and allocated. To deal with such bureaucracy, some social workers report that managers are requesting cases to be processed quickly to meet targets by, for example, 'downgrading' child protection (CP) cases to less urgent child in need (CIN) cases, or, in cases where there is no element of child protection, by declining to offer any social work involvement at all (Stevenson, 2015) However, in her review of child protection in 2011, Eileen Munro signalled a welcomed sea change for system development, making recommendations to move away from a prescriptive child protection system that contributed to past failings towards one with a greater understanding of complexity (Munro, 2011). The review made a series of recommendations, including the loosening of assessment timescales and greater emphasis on the importance of relationship-focused work, professional judgement, decision making and analytical skills. Although assessment timescales were loosened following the Munro review, a subsequent focus on quality assurance, computer systems and crisis intervention (at the expense of funding for staff and services) has hindered the implementation of the other recommendations (Stevenson, 2015). An over-reliance on managerialism still exists, and is arguably stronger than it has ever been, making it more difficult than ever before for social workers effectively to perform their role of safeguarding children. In the current practice climate, heavy workloads, too much bureaucracy and lack of time and resources put social workers under pressure (Stevenson, 2015). Children's safety is compromised by performance-obsessed managerialism and austerity cuts, and not, as some claim, by professional competence or wilful negligence.

Seeking solutions to improving information sharing means that child welfare professionals have had to digest, understand, and adhere to a proliferation of ever-more comprehensive policy guidance and procedures. A bureaucratic 'control and command' regime has emerged for professionals within the web of the child protection system (Munro, 2011) where the imperative has increasingly been about process rather than practice. Child welfare professionals and managers alike will relate to this statement all too well. The raft of reforms and the 'expansionist project' that has ensued since the New Labour government years has been largely remedial; the received notion is that professional competencies and compliance are at fault, and therefore all that professionals within their agencies need to do is to get better at this thing termed 'information sharing' with the assistance of more detailed guidance. Recent messages from high-profile public inquiries show there has been little change in the assumptions that failings in information sharing can be easily remedied. These are, however, erroneous assumptions.

Throughout the New Labour years (1997–2010), and the coalition government's time in office (2010–15), messages from serious case reviews and high-profile public inquiries into the deaths of children such as Peter Connelly (2007), Callum Wilson (2011), Keanu Williams (2011), Daniel Pelka (2012) and Hamzah Khan (2013) continue to find fault with multi-agency working and information sharing among child welfare professionals. In so many instances, this message, coupled with the circumstances of a child's death, becomes the focus of media wrath, vilifying the professionals involved in the child's life. A good example of this is the 'witch hunt' of the professionals involved in the Peter Connelly case. After Peter died, *The Sun* newspaper launched the 'Baby P justice campaign', calling for severe punishment for the professionals involved in the case (Jones, 2014, p 1). Recent calls by David Cameron for the criminalisation of social workers in children's social care only serve to reinforce such unhelpful media messages, which do not assist in any way in the development of a safer child protection system. The recent message that 'failing' services should transform standards or be subject to privatisation (Stevenson, 2015) is also unhelpful; such sentiments do not create meaningful dialogue in addressing the complexity of child protection work, nor what can be learned from child death tragedies in developing a positive, open and honest safety culture for sharing information and generating knowledge across organisational boundaries (White et al, 2015, p 63). Rather, a culture of professional 'blame and shame', driven by the media and the Conservative government, continues to prevail, despite an elusive rhetoric of learning lessons from such tragedies.

In this book it is not my purpose to negate the importance of information sharing in child protection work; nor am I inclined to be critical of, or analytical about, how child welfare professionals perform this task in 'everyday' practices. Rather, I am suggesting that the recommendations of successive public inquiry reports over the decades, while readily given credence because of the emotive context of their dissemination, tend to be circular. The same perceived failings occur time and time again, despite huge investment in e-technologies, guidance, training and procedure attached to this aspect of multi-agency working. This begs a need for a different and alternative focus of enquiry, does it not? Based on findings from my own research data, as well as practising as a childcare social worker at the time of writing this book, I have come to the conclusion that the stock vocabulary of 'information sharing' is considered in far too simplistic terms. Information sharing is a task that needs to be understood in *context*. An over-emphasis on headline-grabbing statements and policy dictates risks undermining some of the very important complexities of how professionals work together to create, share, act on and decipher 'information'. The intention of this book is to show that the policy rhetoric of information sharing, while based on laudable intents, falls short of articulating some of these complexities – these can only come to light when observing and talking to those professionals in their respective fields doing the complex and difficult work of protecting children. I am by no means claiming that this book can provide all the answers in 'fixing' issues in information sharing to prevent all future child fatalities; this would, of course, would be completely naïve and unrealistic. I am certain that I do not have all the answers, or even many of them. However, what I can claim with confidence is this book seeks to offer a *human factors* perspective to the information sharing debate in England and Wales, as well speaking to an international audience in 'Anglophone' countries such as Australia and the US. In addition, I aim to offer support to fellow professionals tasked with safeguarding children by prompting critical reflection and a multi-agency understanding of an activity that is often taken for granted. Thus, the questions used as the basis for enquiry, and addressed in this book, are as follows:

- What can be learnt about information practices from a range of professionals working on the ground who are tasked with protecting children from harm?
- What can professional information behaviours tell us about information-sharing practices?
- What factors prompt other professionals to share information at the referral stage with local authority social workers in children's services?
- How might children's services organise their work differently around the welfare of the child?
- How can understanding the human factors of information sharing contribute to strengthening the child protection system, and improve official responses to future child fatalities?

In addressing these questions, I take a qualitative approach with a particular interest in *practice*. The original research was funded as a case studentship by the Economic and Social Research Council and sponsored by a local authority children's services department in the north of England. The sponsoring local authority had raised concerns about the rise in referral figures in the locality, and the ability to only offer level 4 child protection responses because of difficulties in balancing demand and resources (see Appendix 1 for threshold criteria for receiving a service). Data collected for this book has been influenced by social constructionism and ethnomethodology, drawing on the ethnographic tradition with its emphasis on the 'everyday' orderliness of local and situated practices, and examining the ways in which practices taken for granted work to produce and reproduce professional and organisational realities (Drew and Heritage, 1992; Boden, 1994) as well as 'collect people's account's with the intention of making a different kind of sense, mobilizing concepts and vocabularies they do not have access to' (Murdock, 1997, p 187).

Between 2007 and 2008, non-participant observations of two referral and assessment teams in children's services, documentary analysis and 34 interviews (n=34) were conducted (see Appendix 2 for interview schedule). Interview accounts were gathered from different professionals within their places of work, across social work, health, education, the police, and non-government child welfare organisations identified from the sponsoring local authority's management information technology data as referring most frequently into children's social care within the locality. Thematic analysis (TA) was used to analyse the data, inductively generating the themes that are presented as data chapters in this book. TA is a flexible analytic method in that it is not tied to any particular theoretical or epistemological approach, although it sits very well within a social constructionist persuasion (Braun and Clarke, 2006) with which I align myself. The advantage of TA is that 'results are generally accessible' and 'can be useful for producing qualitative analyses suited to informing policy development'(Braun and Clarke, 2006, p 97), and as such it is considered to be the approach most suited in talking to multi-agency professionals – the intended audience for this research.

A continued issue

The Spanish philosopher Ortega commented that 'every generation has its theme' (Neef, 2008). Such themes are dominated by particular forms of language that often occur as a result of a perceived crisis. Crises in the form of child deaths and successive inquiry reports have led to changes in the language of 'information sharing' and consequently associated micro-management apparatus in safeguarding children. The 'expansionist information-sharing project' has been a continued 'theme' of the past four decades, and I surmise that this theme is not likely to be overturned any time soon. A stock vocabulary has emerged, albeit subject to 'modernisation', and continues to gloss the complexities of 'information sharing' in *practice*, and how this is achieved in the context of organisational and procedural requirements, professional cultures and individual interpretation and understanding. However, there has been little attempt in the context of child protection to tackle some of the most basic questions such as 'What is "information"?' and 'How does "it" work in practice?' How can solutions be sought to improve 'information sharing' when it is not clear what properties formulate or constitute the 'information' that professionals are required to share? Problematically, official legislative, policy and practice documents hold objectivist assumptions about the stability of the meaning of 'information' within child welfare information-sharing activity. While such documents touch on the issue of relativism, whereby different professionals may have a different language to describe what they think is going on in respect of the children and families they work with, policy discourses still assume that each professional, using his/her particular language, can elicit 'information' that is finite, stable, and, vocabulary notwithstanding, mirrors a social world available to all. However, my aim in this book is to show that trying to understand what information *is*, and *how* it works requires a significantly more complex set of ideas than the objectivist assumptions within policy discourses or the suggestions of relativism imply. It is only by taking the 'theme' of 'information sharing' and looking at it through a human factors lens that new questions, possibilities and conversations emerge. In doing so, we can then start to address some fundamental questions such as 'What can be learnt from destabilising the concept of information?', 'How can alternative ways of thinking about information be meaningfully applied in a child welfare context?' and 'How might new ways of understanding information assist in improving collaborative child protection practices?' The chapters in this book seek to address all of these questions and considerations collectively.

Structure of the book

Chapter Two provides a policy and legislative context to 'information sharing' and shows the impact of child deaths and high-profile public inquiries that have been the impetus for an integration agenda, and a key driver for shoring up information-sharing practices. This chapter charts key historical changes that have influenced the role and conceptualisation of 'information' and 'working together', and crucially highlights how 'information' has shifted from being 'part of' the work of child protection to, increasingly, 'the nature' of the work. Chapter

Three offers critical analysis of information sharing, particularly in the context of the referral process, and how information can be thought of differently in this context. The purpose of this chapter is to illustrate what can be learnt from destabilising the concept of 'information', and how alternative ways of thinking about information can meaningfully be applied at an early stage of the information-sharing process. In essence, this chapter indicates that trying to understand what information is and how it works requires a significantly complex set of ideas than is frequently offered through broadly objectivist assumptions within policy discourses. Chapter Four charts new ground by providing a reading of key material drawn from a range of academic disciplines such as complexity science and information science, and thus 'stretches' current conceptualisations of 'information sharing' by introducing 'information behaviour' and professional 'information needs' to the child welfare 'information-sharing' debate. Drawing on interview accounts from a number of professionals in diverse multi-agency settings, Chapter Five illustrates how professionals enact the formal mechanisms of 'information sharing' in everyday practices; it is the bureaucratic, professional 'technical competencies' that are scrutinised retrospectively (that is, focusing on what professionals in their agencies have and have not done) and are persistently considered an area at fault that needs to be remedied. Contrary to received ideas, this chapter highlights high levels of compliance in professional talk with policy, legislative and practice guidance, and therefore begs the question: 'Where is information-sharing practice falling down?' Chapter Six begins to explore this question by examining the 'jigsaw' metaphor, so familiar in practice, of piecing information together to ascertain a 'full picture' of children's lives; this concept is manifest in policy and legislative guidance, although professional accounts demonstrate areas of complexity and a mismatch between the theory and practice of assembling the pieces of a jigsaw to gather a 'full' picture on the ground. Chapter Seven explores the role of relationships. Central to this chapter is drawing out a distinction between inter-personal and inter-professional relationships between people who are required to work together, and perhaps most importantly, relationships with (or not with) information. The idea of information relationships is crucial if we are to get any closer in understanding how matters can get missed, or fail to be prioritised or connected to a case (in other words, where the relationship with information is not achieved). Thus, this chapter goes some way in explaining how it is that calls for better information-sharing practices are not wholly resolved by improving multi-agency working through more detailed guidance and standardisation, training, or merely bringing people together in the same room to discuss a case. Chapter Eight introduces the role of emotions and associated professional information behaviours in information sharing – I term this 'emotion information'. This chapter illustrates that emotions are information in themselves; they influence and shape information-sharing practices in many ways that are not obvious from official guidance, nor can be understood by following traditional lines of enquiry. In exploring emotions in the context of information sharing, this chapter importantly demonstrates how feelings, hunches and uncertainty are 'translated' into information that can be passed on, and how these feelings can influence the meaning secured to information and affect what is recorded, or what is spoken or left unspoken, and so forth; it is emotion information that causes confusion and tension between social workers in local authority children's services and other child welfare professionals by 'rewriting' what the concerns are. In fact, the referral information that social workers often have to deal with is the 'by-product' of the collective emotions of other child welfare professionals. Finally, the concluding chapter pulls together the main threads discussed earlier in order to extend the current information-sharing dialogue and move the debate forward with its inherent complexities intact.

TWO

The significance of 'information sharing' in safeguarding children

Introduction

As a result of a number of high-profile public inquiries into the tragic deaths of children spanning more than four decades, 'information sharing' has now become a moral and political imperative for improving the welfare and protection of children. Children's services in England and Wales have become increasingly 'integrated' in that agencies in health, welfare, education, criminal justice and housing are tasked with working more closely together to support families and safeguard children. While the language of 'working together' and 'joined-up services', and the concept of the 'co-located' professional whose work transcends and cuts across traditional boundaries are most readily associated with previous New Labour administrations, the idea that agencies need to work together effectively to meet the needs of children and families is not new. Arrangements for coordinating services for children can be attributed to a circular issued in 1950, which, in response to the ill treatment of children, recommended the establishment of children's coordinating committees (Home Office, cited in Hallett and Stevenson, 1980). Over a decade later in 1968, the Seebohm report recommended the formation of unified social services departments that were to be derived from the 'joining up' of local authority children's health and welfare departments, so that services for individuals, children, families and communities might be rendered more effective. Aside from this report, it was the death of a seven-year-old girl, Maria Colwell, at the hands of her step-father William Kepple in 1973, and the subsequent committee inquiry to investigate the circumstances of her death, that progressed the notion of integrated service delivery, placing 'working together' firmly on the policy agenda in regard to dealing with non-accidental injury to children (DHSS, 1974).

Maria Colwell, born in March 1965 in Hove, was the youngest of five children. Within weeks of Maria's birth, her father, Raymond Colwell, left the family home, and some months later, when Maria was nearly four months old, died of natural causes, leaving Pauline Colwell (Maria's mother) with sole care of their five children. As she was unable to cope with the situation, Pauline Colwell initiated plans to send Maria to live with her late husband's sister, Doris Cooper. In response to child protection concerns, the four remaining children were removed from Pauline's care under legislation equivalent to a care order today. Significantly, in 1966, Pauline Colwell met William Kepple (Maria's step-father), whom she later married. In October 1971, the local authority reluctantly returned Maria to the care of her mother, a home in which Mr Kepple was also living (Butler and Drakeford, 2003, p 84). Maria was seen over 50 times before her death by a number of professionals from different agencies. On 7 January 1973, Maria was taken to hospital in a pram by her mother and step-father where she was pronounced dead; she had suffered brain damage, a fractured rib, black eyes, extensive external bruising and internal injuries. The pathologist described Maria's case as "the worst he had ever seen" and her injuries as resulting from "extreme violence" (cited in Butler and Drakeford, 2003, p 85). Maria's step-father, William Kepple, was convicted of Maria's murder (a charge that was later reduced to manslaughter) in April 1973.

The death of Maria has been regarded as historically significant in that it laid the foundations for a child protection system that professionals are familiar with today (Parton, 1985). The inquiry report into Maria's death significantly brought to the fore the lack of, or weaknesses in, cooperation between services (in particular schools, education welfare and social services), and in the way professionals worked together and shared information (Colwell Report, 1974, pp 67-8); indeed, these concerns still resonate and have had relevance in successive inquiry reports to date. It is thus important to turn to a series of public inquiries into the deaths of children to chart the growing significance of information sharing in child protection legislation, policy and practice, in which there has been a growing shift from 'social' work to the 'informational' (Parton, 2008), and the need for professionals to work together more closely and effectively in meeting the demands of the 'informational turn'.

Shaping the child protection system: messages from public inquiries

In investigating the circumstances surrounding Maria Colwell's death, and commenting on the existing child protection system, the report committee identified 'many failures of communication' (Colwell Report, 1974, para 149, p 61) and information sharing. The report committee noted:

> While we entirely accept that a heavy responsibility for passing on and eliciting information to these 'other agencies' rests on social services departments, we must nonetheless stress that this should not be a one way process and that social workers may reasonably expect that matters of concern about individual families or children will be passed on to them by these agencies whether or not they have already indicated their interest to them. The problem of communication is a complex one, resting as it does on a combination of formal and informal arrangements, of administrative systems and direct personal contact. But in view of the fact that Maria, despite an elaborate system of 'welfare provisions', fell through the net primarily because of communication failures, we feel it helpful to discuss in some detail the implications for 'the other agencies' of the points at which, in our views, serious flaws in the information flow to the social services departments occurred. (Colwell Report, 1974, para 152, p 62)

The report committee drew attention to 'serious flaws in the information flow' between other professionals and social services departments. Maria was known to a number of agencies, including two local authority social services departments, as well as her school, the NSPCC and the housing department (Munro, 2005). Each of these agencies had some concerns about Maria's welfare, although their understandings were confined to a partial picture of her life, due to limited information held by each agency, which consequently did not reflect the significance and severity of the problems Maria encountered in her life. One of the key lessons learnt from the inquiry report was the importance of professionals sharing information so that an accurate and fuller picture of a child's life could be formulated (Munro, 2005, p 377).

The inquiry report into Maria's death stimulated a number of key changes to improve the child protection system, and notably, led to the circular by the Department of Health and Social Security (DHSS) entitled *Non accidental injury to children* (DHSS, 1974), which replaced earlier guidance on battered babies (DHSS, 1970, 1972). These publications prompted the need to develop a child protection system that would ensure that professionals from key agencies could first, identify signs of non-accidental injury to children, and second, create a better system that would facilitate improved information sharing between professionals. In response to these publications, draft guidelines making recommendations for improving multi-agency coordination were published (Corby, 2006), and systems put in place so that information could be shared between professionals such as health visitors, GPs and the police, with social workers tasked as coordinators of the work. The mechanisms of area review committees and child protection conferences (now known as case conferences) were implemented to facilitate the bringing together of professionals to share information about child protection concerns, make decisions based on the information shared, and monitor and review those concerns in terms of observable and measurable progress. At the same time, the 'child protection register' (now a child protection plan) was also to be implemented (Hudson, 2005a, 2005b) – a means by which professionals could establish whether the child was already known to be at risk of maltreatment.

In the 1980s, a series of highly publicised child deaths pointed to the incompleteness of the Colwell reforms. The tragic deaths of Lucy Gates (London Borough of Bexley, 1982), Jasmine Beckford (London Borough of Brent, 1985) and Tyra Henry (London Borough of Lambeth, 1987) illuminated the continued inadequacies of the child protection system. As a result of these tragedies, albeit speculatively, it was during this decade that the familiar concept of child 'abuse', comprising the sub-categories of physical injury, emotional abuse, physical neglect and a child's failure to thrive, became a 'certified' and political phenomenon that professionals were required to recognise, and respond to effectively in coordinated ways.

The public inquiry into the death of four-year-old Jasmine Beckford in 1985, similar to the Maria Colwell inquiry report, drew attention to inadequacies in the collaboration between health and social services. The aims of the Jasmine Beckford report, however, were threefold: first, to raise awareness of child 'abuse' and in particular the 'risk' of child 'abuse'; second, to ensure that any allegation of child 'abuse' was swiftly responded to; and third, to stimulate further development of systems to improve inter-agency cooperation that would monitor children deemed to be at risk (Corby, 2006). Area review committees were replaced by area child protection committees (DHSS and Welsh Office, 1988), whose primary role was to coordinate the work of local agencies, develop and deliver inter-professional training, and produce local protocols detailing what procedures should be followed by professionals if a child had been abused, or they suspected that a child was at risk of being abused. The concept of risk spread the information net – the need to share information on a much wider range of signs and symptoms became salient.

Significantly, the underlying message echoed in the Beckford report shifted the core attention to the 'child' and their need for protection and away from the needs and rights of parents. It was through the Beckford report that children were reframed not as victims, but as *potential* victims of child 'abuse', in parallel to the notion that parents were *potential* child 'abusers' (Corby, 2006).

This received idea served to underline the important role for professionals in 'detecting' and 'reporting' potential child 'abuse', with communication across organisational boundaries and the sharing of information as central to this professional work.

The Beckford inquiry report seemingly created repercussions for social work practice, namely a significant increase in the numbers of children placed on the child protection register (now referred to as a child protection plan) from 1985 onwards (Corby, 2006). The proceeding events in Cleveland in 1987 placed child sexual abuse firmly on the child protection agenda. The 'Cleveland child sex abuse scandal' placed the notion of child 'abuse' firmly in the minds of professionals and the public alike, serving as a warrant for public intervention into the lives of families, and the sharing of 'private' information. The publication of the Jasmine Beckford inquiry report and the publicity that surrounded it prompted Cleveland social service departments to review their childcare strategy, with emphasis placed on ensuring that they would not make mistakes (similar to those in the Beckford case) that would result in children being 'unavoidably abused' (DH, 1988, p 56). However, the events of Cleveland saw (what some considered to be) the over-zealous removal of children from their homes. As a consequence, and what was a very different message from previous public inquiries, social workers were publically criticised for excessive and unwarranted intrusion into family life (Parton, 1991). Thus, social workers found themselves in a situation of equal proportions in which they were dammed if they did, and dammed if they didn't.

Beginning the formalisation process of 'working together' and 'information sharing'

The publication of the Cleveland report in 1988 (DH, 1988), and previously the report into tragic death of Kimberley Carlile in 1986 (London Borough of Greenwich, 1987), importantly led to the publication of the first *Working together* guidelines for professionals. The new 'how to' guide, entitled *Working together: A guide to arrangements for inter-agency co-operation for the protection of children from abuse* (DHSS and Welsh Office, 1988), made the process of working together into a formalised procedure for jointly protecting children from maltreatment, and also officially extended the definition of child 'abuse' to include sexual abuse, as a result of the Cleveland case. These first formalised guidelines for working together were contained in an A5, 72-page pamphlet detailing how professionals should cooperate to protect children from 'abuse'. As stated in Part One, para 1.3:

> [A]ll agencies have specific functions and professional objectives. In working together for the protection of children, however, they need to understand that they are not only carrying out their own agency's functions but are also making, individually and collectively, a vital contribution to advising and assisting the local authority in the discharge of its child protection and child care duties. **Therefore it is essential that wherever one agency becomes concerned that a child may be at risk they share their information with other agencies** as other agencies may have information which will clarify the situation. (DHSS and Welsh Office, 1988, p 6; emphasis in original)

Exchanging information between agencies is seen as a key aspect of this version of working together. Part Five of the same document provides a dedicated section entitled 'Exchange of information', which outlines that agencies are required to make concerted efforts to share and exchange 'relevant' information with social services or the NSPCC. However, it is not made clear in this first edition of *Working together* what 'relevant' information consists of. Already, in the first definitive document, we can see some of the problems in trying to delineate professional and procedural activities with respect to information sharing. For the first time professionals were being commanded to share information without any clear remit as to what that information might be. It was assumed that child 'abuse' (and the risk of it) would be self-evident following clear signs and symptoms, as professionals were led to believe through the evidence of Professor Cyril Greenland, a professor of social work at McMaster University, Canada to the Beckford inquiry

In the wake of significant professional and media interest in child 'abuse', an important review of childcare law took place, resulting in the development of the Children Act 1989. The Act sought to achieve a balance between the protection of children and support for families, avoiding unwarranted intrusion into family life (Parton, 1991). Under Part III, Section 17 of the Act, preventative services could be offered to support families in caring for children in need, and to promote the welfare of such children. However, with its focus on the general duty of local authorities to safeguard the welfare of children within their area, the Act reinforced the legitimacy of local authority intervention into private family life under Section 47, the criteria for which are based on whether the child is 'suffering, or likely to suffer significant harm' (Section 31(9), (10); Section 47(1)). Under Section 27 of the Act, local authorities could request help from other named authorities (health, education, housing, or another local authority) to facilitate the sharing of information between authorities about children in need.

In taking into account the implementation of the Children Act 1989, the government followed with the publication of the second *Working together* practice guidance in 1991. This guidance, entitled *Working together to safeguard children: A guide to arrangements for inter-agency cooperation for the protection of children from abuse* expanded the original first *Working together* guidelines from a 72-page, A5 pamphlet to a 126-page A4 book. The mere extension of the guidelines illustrated the increased significance that working together was playing in the professional work of protecting children from 'abuse'. This second publication (Home Office et al, 1991) outlined the need for greater, measurable, planned and coordinated responses (Corby, 2006). Again, similar to the first *Working together* publication, familiar themes relating to information sharing were reiterated. The successful delivery of joint working depended on information sharing, collaboration between professionals, and an understanding of respective agency roles (Home Office et al, 1991, pp 2-3). In this edition of *Working together*, the term 'crucially' preceded 'effective information sharing', illustrating the growing significance of information sharing in the child welfare agenda, and it becoming an essential prerequisite in effectively protecting children from harm. Furthermore, it is in this edition that explicit suggestions are made about information sharing at the stage of referral. The publication states that anyone (whether a professional or a member of the public) who has cause to suspect that a child is suffering or at risk of suffering significant harm should refer their concerns to agencies that have statutory obligations to intervene. In the majority of cases, this is children's social care agencies. The report also introduced the notions of professional skills, expertise and competencies in effective communication, coordination and cooperation. Respectively, it is stated that social workers, health visitors, child health doctors, GPs, police officers, and the NSPCC should be the agencies that are 'particularly involved in the process of gathering what is deemed "relevant" information and carrying forward the work with a child and family' (Home Office et al, 1991, p 27). Reference is simply made to 'relevant information', without further expansion or explanation for professionals. Thus, it is taken for granted that professionals will know what information is deemed relevant, without any explanation of what this type of information means or consists of.

The implementation of *Working together* guidance for improved information sharing failed to remedy past failings of the child protection system. While the 1989 Children Act and the subsequent *Working together* practice guidance (Home Office et al, 1991) clearly provided the statute and procedure for working together and information sharing, a report published by the Audit Commission in 1994 once again drew attention to failures in the child protection system. While this report was based on a number of different themes and analyses, central to the report, and encapsulated in the title *Seen but not heard*, was a concern with the interface between health and social care, which highlighted the plight of children with disabilities and those in the most need. While the focus was on children in need and children with disabilities, once again the report drew attention to that lack of effective coordination and information sharing between services, which consequently resulted in children slipping through the net.

Following the events in Cleveland, the government commissioned over 20 research projects, the findings of which were published under the title *Child protection: Messages from research* (DH, 1995). These studies reviewed child protection services with the aim of establishing the impact of the Children Act 1989, and associated policy and practice developments. This document delivered messages about the continued failure of child protection services to deliver services for the broader population of children in need. Findings suggested that partnership with families was poorly developed, and that long-term inter-agency work was not effective beyond the point of investigation. The effect of the publication was to prompt a national debate led by the Department of Health that has become known as the 're-focusing debate' (Parton, 1998). The core of this debate centred on how services could be delivered or redefined in such a way that they would be experienced more positively, and that that would then enable more children to receive services. This debate is seen to have effected something of a paradigm shift from child protection to child welfare, with the notion of family 'support' re-emerging as a central practice imperative. As such, emphasis was placed on ensuring that statutory intervention was not only a route to services, but that there was also adequate response/provision for children 'in need' (DH, 1995; Parton, 1998). Reconceptualising the relationship between family support and child protection in the 1990s can be seen as very different compared with the emphasis on policy and practice from the mid-1970s onwards when forensic 'evidence' and the importance of investigation was key (Wattam, 1992; Parton, 1997). Nevertheless, attempting to deliver a less 'punitive' response to families did not remove the need for effective communication from the child welfare agenda.

In light of *Child protection: Messages from research* (DH, 1995) and the 'refocusing debate' (Parton, 1998), *Working together* guidelines were again revised and published in 1999 (DH et al, 1999). This edition was coupled with the introduction of the *Framework for the assessment of children in need and their families* (Department of Health, Home Office, and Department of Education and Employment, 2000) and replaced the former 'Orange Book' (DH, 1988). Similar to *Working together* guidance, the assessment framework was issued under Section 7 of the Local Authority Social Services Act 1970, meaning that both guidance documents were required to be followed unless professionals could give good reasons for not doing so.

The third edition of *Working together* is interesting insofar as a change in title and language occurred. This edition was entitled *Working together to safeguard children: A guide to inter-agency working to safeguard and promote the welfare of children* (DH et al, 1999). In this 119-page edition, terms such as 'abuse' are omitted from the title, and 'protection' is replaced with the central concept of the document: 'safeguarding'. The term 'safeguarding' was an important feature under Section 17 of the Children Act 1989, although its meaning within this legislative framework was not made entirely clear. In lacking a proper definition, the term was open to varying interpretations (Ofsted, 2005). It is also in this third edition that the term 'an integrated approach' is introduced for the first time. It appears to replace frequently used terms such as 'cooperate' and 'coordinate'. A move away from the latter terms towards 'integration' implied a shift away from professionals being brought together in a voluntary action, and towards providing a more controlled, 'seamless' way of working and delivering services. It is also in this edition that the introduction of 'promoting children's welfare' first appears as part of the working together agenda, and thus 'working together' sees a shift from protecting children from abuse, to working with prevention, and extended categories of need.

In charting the historical policy and legislative developments for improving the child protection system thus far, there is no doubt that under previous New Labour administrations 'working together' had been placed firmly in the spotlight. Politically, there were a number of reasons for this; it was not incidental, but deliberate. Early in office in 1997, New Labour made a clear and somewhat ambitious commitment to eradicating child poverty by 2012, and the associated issue of social exclusion. The development of the term 'safeguarding' children was purported to extend understandings of child protection, with factors such as social exclusion, domestic violence, drug and alcohol dependency, and the mental health of parents or carers being considered detrimental to children's welfare (Cleaver et al, 1999). These, together with drawing attention to the multi-faceted nature of deprivation and disadvantage, led the then newly elected government to call for 'joined-up solutions'. New Labour also drew attention to the increasing complexity of family life due to social change, identifying that families today face a number of problems that require that agencies work together. By placing social exclusion on the political agenda, and thus widening understandings about what constitutes detriment to children, the safeguarding agenda became as much about maximising inclusion as it was about minimising harm to children (Axford, 2008), and therefore required wider-ranging multi-agency responses.

'Every child matters' and the 'informational turn'

At the dawn of the millennium, the serious maltreatment and eventual death of an eight-year-old girl named Anna (later known as Victoria) Climbié came to light. Before her death, Victoria was known to many local authority children's social care departments, the health service and the police, as the following quote notes:

> Eight-year old Victoria died in February 2000 from hypothermia, malnutrition and physical abuse suffered at the hands of her carer, a great aunt and her cohabite. Over a 10-month period, Victoria had been known to the social services of four local authorities and two police child protection teams, as well as admitted with non-accidental injuries to the paediatric wards of two different hospitals within the space of 10 days. (Reder and Duncan, p 84)

In a similar vein to previous inquiries, the inquiry chaired by Lord Laming into the death of Victoria Climbié sought to establish the circumstances surrounding the death surrounding the death of Victoria Climbié, to reach conclusions, and offer recommendations to avoid such tragic events happening to future children. The inquiry lasted 20 months; a total of 4,000 documents were read, and 277 witnesses gathered (Masson,

2006). Laming's final report was over 400 pages long, and included 108 recommendations for government to consider for improving the child protection system (Laming, 2003). In his report, Laming concluded that there had been 'gross failure of the system' as a result of 'widespread organisational malaise' (Masson, 2006, p 221).

The public and the media articulated total dismay that the agencies involved failed to take action to protect Victoria, despite the 'unmistakeable' signs of physical maltreatment that she had endured at the hands of her aunt and her aunt's partner. Fuelled with these perceptions, the media and the public alike blamed the professionals involved for these insuperable errors. The death of Victoria Climbié is often seen as the catalyst for closer cooperation and greater information-sharing practices between professional agencies, and thus, the impact of Victoria's death and the Climbié inquiry report that followed is significant. Like previous high-profile inquiries into non-accidental child deaths, the Climbié inquiry once again drew very clear attention to failings in local authorities to 'work together', highlighting that the formalisation of 'working together' to facilitate greater information sharing for improving the child protection system was far from being adequately resolved.

Following Victoria's death, the powerful appellation 'every child matters' (ECM) configured under New Labour placed inter-professional practice at the heart of the policy agenda for children, and became an overarching principle for working with children and their families. The ECM agenda was initially introduced as a Green Paper (DfES, 2003), and was to herald what has been seen as the most ambitious reform ever of children's services (Laming, 2003). It has been suggested that ECM created 'the biggest shake up since the Seebohm report of the 1960s' (Williams, 2004, p 406).

Indeed, what emerged under the guise of ECM was that despite very significant and repeated attempts to tackle failings in information sharing following earlier public inquiries, there was still further need to improve inter-agency communication. In this context, Laming's solution to integrate services (underpinned by greater information sharing) to safeguard children and young people in the future became a justified and necessary response.

ECM proposed the establishment of local children's safeguarding boards, responsible for safeguarding children, the implementation of which would extend the executive-level decision-making and training responsibility of area child protection committees, but increase their role in the regulation and audit of child protection responses. Furthermore, commitment to 'joint working' was also underpinned by the introduction of children's trust arrangements that would be supported by central government and was seen as a way to oversee the development of local procedures and to increase collaboration between frontline workers (Cleaver et al, 2004). In its overall aims, the publication of the Green Paper *Every child matters* (Department for Education, 2003) formalised Laming's request for integrated service delivery, and more importantly, reinforced the need for radical child welfare reform and cultural change:

> Improving outcomes for children and young people, so that every child achieves their potential, involves changes to culture and practices across the children's workforce.... Integrated working focuses on enabling and encouraging professionals to work together and to adopt common processes to deliver frontline services, coordinated and built around the needs of children and young people. (Gray et al, 2012, p 214)

Thus, in the aftermath of the Victoria Climbié inquiry, the proposed new ways of working found broad appeal, despite their (over)ambition. Peckover and colleagues sophistically augment:

> The appellation 'Every Child Matters' applied to both the Green Paper and the Children Act 2004 offers an incontrovertible moral imperative. Who could possibly dispute that *every child matters*? Thus the reforms have drawn upon a linguistic repertoire that constructs the changes as an ethical imperative for professionals working with children and young people. (2008, p 378)

The agenda of ECM, in aiming to ensure that no child would slip through the net of preventative services, outlined a model with a far broader scope of support to families – introducing the category of children with 'additional needs' and drawing universal services far more closely together in the work of supporting families and safeguarding children. This broad agenda was reflected in the five outcome statements detailed within the first Green Paper: being healthy, staying safe, enjoying and achieving, making a positive contribution, and economic well-being (DfES, 2003); this was reflected in a definition of safeguarding:

> The process of protecting children from abuse and neglect, preventing impairment or [sic] their health and development, and ensuring that they are growing up in circumstances consistent with the provision of safe and effective care that enables children to have optimum life chances and enter adulthood successfully. (Ofsted, 2008, p 3)

The establishment of an all-encompassing way of working, endorsed by the appellation 'every child matters', undeniably legitimised the progression of surveillance practices that might otherwise have been more widely contested (Penna, 2005). Lyon (2001, p 2) defines the term 'surveillance' as 'any collection and processing of personal data, where identifiable or not, for the purposes of influencing or managing those whose data has been garnered'. More specifically, Lyon (1988, p 96) advocates that 'the mundane reality is that everyday information becomes the basis of much "surveillance"'. Thus, in terms of the information demands of a broader, more universal approach, the New Labour government produced the policy documents: *Every child matters: Next steps* (DfES, 2004a) and *Every child matters: Change for children* (DfES, 2004b), detailing an integrated approach to promoting the wellbeing of children and young people.

In the same year, the Children Act 2004 was passed to support the ECM agenda for developing more effective and accessible services, focused around the needs of children, young people and families (DfES, 2004a). This Act may be regarded as a landmark piece of legislation with regard to its ambitions to facilitate information sharing, and to further break down potential barriers to information flows. Under Sections 10 and 11 of the Children Act 2004, local authorities and key partners now had a duty to cooperate in promoting and protecting the wellbeing of children. In other words, the Children Act 2004 emphasised the statutory obligations of professionals assuming responsibility for safeguarding children (Goldthorpe, 2004). This was also assumed under the Children Act 1989, and was supported by *Every child matters* (DfES, 2003), and the Laming inquiry (Laming, 2003). However, under the 2004 Act, professionals from a variety of agencies were now tasked with safeguarding responsibility, with a duty to disclose information where failure to do so would result in a child or children suffering child maltreatment. In general terms, the law no longer prevented information sharing with other professionals to assist in safeguarding a child if:

• those likely to be affected consent;
• the public interest in safeguarding the child's welfare overrides the need to keep the information confidential;
• disclosure is required under a court order or other legal obligation.

Policy and legislative developments meant that key agencies were no longer 'detectors' or 'reporters' of problems for social services. Instead, if families were known to agencies, they were thought to occupy a pivotal role in working in partnership with families to find resolutions to problems before they reached crisis point (DfES, 2004b). As such, the modernisation of children's services transformed the safeguarding of children into 'everybody's business', through broadening professional accountability and foregrounding information sharing as a means of achieving such aims. Furthermore, it reclassified the safeguarding task as protecting children and young people from failing to reach their maximum 'potential' (Penna, 2005). In doing so, Williams (2004), in her commentary on *Every child matters*, noted that the ECM guidance was heavily weighted towards statutory interventions that monitor and reinforce parental responsibilities, but less so towards providing parental participation and support (p 417).

Post-Climbié and e-technology developments

Information failings were again brought to the fore in the context of the Bichard report (2004) following the death of two schoolgirls, Jessica Chapman and Holly Wells, in Soham at the hands of Ian Huntley, a man who was previously known to the police in another county as a suspected serial sex offender, but irrespective of this, was employed as a caretaker at the girls' school. The schoolgirls' deaths, which highlighted the inability of other agencies to access the national police database (Hudson, 2005a, p 539), further supported the development of the information sharing and assessment (ISA) project proposed within the ECM agenda. Its intention was to address this kind of problem by improving information sharing, under Section 12 of the Children Act 2004, which authorised local authorities and their partners to create, and maintain, a database for children in their areas. In the House of Lords, Baroness Ashton articulated the role that such a database might have played in preventing earlier child deaths: 'I believe that this system might have helped Victoria Climbié. It might have saved her life' (*Hansard*, 25.05.04, col. 1160, cited in Munro, 2005, 375). The considered benefits of the index would thus '[E]nable professionals delivering services to children to identify and contact one another easily and quickly, so they can share relevant information about children who need services or about whose welfare they are concerned' (Gutherson and Pickard, 2007, p 3).

A key strand of the ISA was the integrated children's system (ICS), which built on existing developments, such as the assessment framework and the looked after children system. ICS was developed to assist professionals to improve outcomes for children in need in their area by facilitating greater information sharing between agencies. The implementation of ICS could be seen as a 'high point' in the move to the 'informational' in children's services. Its electronic infrastructure was seen as offering a distinct approach to undertaking key tasks of assessment, planning, intervention and reviewing, with consideration given to children's developmental needs in the context of their families and communities (Penna, 2005), increasingly shaping the way that services respond to complex needs (Shaw et al, 2009). However, the introduction of ICS meant that the typical understanding and process of 'making a referral' changed subtly but significantly, the difference being the emergence of a 'contact' that became the first stage of the initial assessment process. From a statistical standpoint, the system was also thought to ensure that local authorities would have the facility to collect requisite information relating to children's services such as the performance assessment framework and quality protects management action plans. In addition to ICS, further 'technological benefits' appeared: ContactPoint and the electronic common assessment framework (eCAF), which were considered key strands of the new integrated system.

The ISA project placed a requirement on each local authority to establish a local information hub (the national version becoming known as ContactPoint) containing basic details on each child from 0-19 in their area. The children's database was originally designed to deal with antisocial behaviour and social exclusion rather than being concerned with protecting children from abuse (Parton, 2006a, pp 149-50). Nevertheless, ContactPoint's intended purpose was to hold basic information about 11 million children in England and Wales, allowing all professionals with access to the database to flag up concerns. In supporting this endeavour, in 2005 Beverley Hughes, the then children's minister, stated:

> There was always a danger that the launch of something called the Information Sharing Index [ContactPoint] would be technical and dispassionate. But Lord Laming has characteristically reminded us in the most human terms what this is really all about: children – their wellbeing, their safety and their care. And I am most grateful to Herbert [Lord Laming] for being here and speaking in those terms. He is here, as are you and I, because we all care passionately about children – their security, happiness and their chances…We've seen the tragic consequences that

failure to share information, or develop a complete picture of a child's circumstances and needs, can have.... (*Hansard*, 2005, cited in Peckover et al, 2008, p 376)

The rationale of an e-government agenda and the implementation of such technology to support the political endeavour were considered to be ways to reduce variability, uncertainty and error in professional performance by facilitating standardised information recording and sharing practices. Unsurprisingly, however, the children's database was not without its contention for a number of reasons: first, because of the mixed success of the 11 local 'trailblazer' authorities in implementing the database and the notable differences in the respective IT applications and their levels of complexity, format, coverage and consent requirements (Cleaver et al, 2004); and second, in respect of a number of commentaries in relation to issues of confidentiality, consent, use of the system, cost and lack of evidence about whether it was the most appropriate way to improve services (House of Commons Education and Skills Committee, 2005; Hudson, 2005a; Munro, 2005; Penna, 2005; Peckover et al, 2008). Nevertheless, as the earlier quote by Beverley Hughes highlights, there was an emotive and moral rationale for developing a database, which drew on the tragic consequences – namely, death – of the failure to share information or build up a 'complete picture' of a child's circumstances. Most notably, Reder and Duncan (2003) retrospectively highlighted that in the majority of public inquiries, professionals have failed to gain a 'full picture' of a child's life, either because certain information was lacking, or because professionals did not actively seek information beyond their own involvement in a case.

A further feature of the e-modernisation agenda, and considered a means to help establish a 'fuller' picture, was the development of the common assessment framework (CAF) as a single assessment tool. The CAF was also considered a means to integrate service responses to children with 'additional' needs. More broadly, the proposal of the CAF arose from concerns that '[t]he existing arrangements for identifying and responding to the needs of children who are not achieving the five outcomes identified in "Every Child Matters" do not work as effectively as they might' (DfES, 2004c, p 6).

The CAF, underpinned by the *Framework for assessment of children in need and their families* (DH et al, 2000), was designed to be used by any professional, irrespective of agency, at the early stages of reporting vulnerability of a child or 'additional' needs', used in cases where child 'abuse' is not the identified concern (Munro, 2005). The new apparatus sought to address problems of information-sharing and communication failures through the lens of prevention, by the development of a 'shared or common language of need/concern' (DCSF, 2007), although this was arguably an ambitious aim, given the different vocabularies and organisational relevancies of agencies (May-Chahal and Broadhurst, 2006). The use of the adjective 'common' was the defining feature of the new processes, with guidance suggesting that the assessment framework 'belongs equally to more than one sector' working with children and families (Warren House Group Dartington Social Research Unit, 2004). Thus, broadening the responsibility of safeguarding across organisational boundaries was again being echoed through calls for effective joint working.

Further *Working together* guidelines were published in 2006 (HM Government, 2006a), updated to take into account the death of Victoria Climbié and the changes prompted by ECM. This guidance echoed the message of prevention, while at the same time strengthening the protection of children (Parton, 2006b). The content of this edition doubled in size from the previous edition and ran to some 256 pages. This fourth edition took quite a different tone from previous editions. Words like 'responsibility' and 'obligation' frequently replaced 'voluntary-toned' words such as 'arrangements'. It is in this version of guidance that information sharing was made even more explicit, emphasising the relationship between flows of information and professional accountability. For example, professionals were being instructed to always consider sharing information; if they failed to share information, they were required to have valid reasons, and furthermore, to record these reasons clearly and accurately.

Bringing the referral process into the political spotlight

One aspect of safeguarding that was largely ignored in the dialect of information sharing until the Laming report in 2003 was the referral process; it was this report that brought the referral process into the political spotlight. Laming identified systemic issues in managing shared information at this point in the child protection process. In April 1999, Victoria's great-aunt Marie-Thérèse Kouao sought housing from various local authorities but was refused as she did not meet the homeless eligibility criteria; a referral from housing was made to social services. A series of further referrals were made to social services following child protection concerns. The alarm was first raised anonymously, but later was known to have come from a Ms Ackah, a family friend. There followed two referrals as a result of admissions to two separate hospitals, after Victoria had been found to have sustained injuries. Finally, in November 1999, Ms Kouao herself alleged that Victoria had been sexually abused. The Laming report identified that the administrative systems for tracking referrals and case information were extremely poor (Laming, 2003). Thus for the first time, and taking into account the findings from the Climbie´ inquiry, the fourth edition of *Working together* (HM Government, 2006a) dedicated an entire section to referrals, both in terms of professional referrals and concerns raised by members of the public with local authority children's social care services. The formalisation of the referral process now made explicit the format for making a referral, the circumstances under which it is appropriate to make a referral to social care, and the requirements on local authority for acknowledging receipt of referrals. It was thus made very clear in 2006 that referrals were finally to be regarded as an important strand of information sharing. Until this point, the referral process had largely been ignored. However, Wattam (1996), in responding to *Child protection: Messages from research* (DH, 1995), put the role of referrals on the child welfare agenda through her ethnographic research, by critiquing the absence of referrals from interrogation. Referrals were considered self-evidential, a necessary evil for reporting concerns of child maltreatment and requesting services. In essence, referrals stood for themselves.

However, Wattam's insightful interrogation of making a case in child protection from referral onwards (Platt, 2006) was arguably never really given the political recognition that it deserved at the time, and it took the tragic death of another child to highlight the significance of referrals. This was not the end of the story. The tragic death of another child, Peter Connelly, in 2007 again brought the referral process, and more broadly information sharing, back to the political fore.

Post-modernisation: the effectiveness of the Climbié reforms

Peter Connelly was 17 months old when he was killed; his mother, Tracey Connelly, her partner and their lodger were convicted in November 2008 of causing or allowing his death. He died as a result of a blow to his head which knocked out one of his teeth, later found in his stomach. The post-mortem report identified that he had a broken back, several rib fractures, multiple bruising and other reported lesions. Peter was subject to a child protection plan with Haringey, the local authority that had been at the centre of public and media scrutiny following the death of Victoria Climbié in 2000. It was reported that Peter had had over 60 contacts with a variety of health and social care professionals before his death, and was pronounced dead within just 48 hours after seeing a hospital paediatrician who had failed to detect that he had a broken spine. In the second serious case review (SCR), it was noted that prior to Peter's death, his family GP had had child protection concerns, but did not share them with other professionals because 'he assumed that others would be in a better position to take action' (Haringey LSCB, 2009, p 21). Evidently, the GP assumed that another professional would be aware of the information he held and equally would share his concern, but would be better placed to take an appropriate course of action. This assumption, and the failure to share information, had consequential effects. Importantly, the GP assumed that if he did not act (share information about his concerns), someone else would. This is a key point for reference – the assumption that someone else will act if many others are involved may lead to inaction by all those concerned.

In response to Peter Connelly's death, the Secretary of State requested that Lord Laming carry out an expedient report on the progress that had been made in England for safeguarding children since the modernisation of services that had taken place after the death of Victoria Climbié. In his report, published in March 2009, Laming commented that:

> It is clear that most staff in social work, youth work, education, police, health, and other frontline services are committed to the principle of inter-agency working, and recognise that children can only be protected effectively when all agencies pool information, expertise, and resources so that a full picture of the child's life is better understood. (Laming, 2009, p 36)

Laming concluded that although positive steps had been made since the modernisation reforms, a lot more needed to be done to improve the child protection system. In the above extract, Laming notes that professionals from a range of agencies share the view of official government discourse that 'working together' and 'information sharing' is essential for the effective protection of children. Expressing similar sentiments to those in the Climbié report (Laming, 2003), Laming drew on assembling a 'full' picture so that professionals are able to better understand the lives of children in order that they be effectively protected. Thus, in the pursuit of a 'full' picture, information from a variety of multi-agency professionals is expected to be *pieced* together.

In light of Peter Connelly's death, the government responded to Lord Laming's report with an action plan on the protection of children in England and Wales (Laming, 2009), and accepted all of Laming's 58 recommendations. Once again, it made reference to effective information sharing, and the importance of delivering more efficient services coordinated around the needs of children. As such, emphasis was placed on embedding information-sharing guidance in training and education and implementing consistent frameworks to support 'good' practice in information sharing. Also contained in this report was a recommendation (reference number 19) stating that all professional referrals to children's services should lead to an initial assessment, with feedback given to the referring professional. *Working together* guidelines were again revised and redrafted in light of 17 recommendations made by Laming. The subsequent, fifth, publication was published in March 2010 (HM Government, 2010a), bearing the same title as the 1999 and 2006 editions, although it had expanded from 231 pages to 393 pages, and had become more complicated, by making reference to further pieces of supplementary guidance that professionals should consult.[1]

The SCR into the death of Khyra Ishaq was published in July 2010, (Birmingham LSCB, 2010) following the fifth edition of *Working together* guidance (HM Government, 2010a). Unsurprisingly, this review brought professional failings in information sharing back into the media spotlight. Khyra was pronounced dead just 20 minutes after arriving at an Accident and Emergency department on 17 May 2008. Khyra was described as severely malnourished, with severe wasting as a result of months of significant starvation. Her mother and her mother's partner were convicted of causing and allowing the death of a child, as well as offences of child cruelty in relation to Khyra's five siblings in March 2010. The SCR highlighted similar findings to those of previous inquiry reports, in that information relating to concerns for Khyra and her siblings' welfare was known to several agencies, and although opportunities for information sharing existed, information was either not recognised or shared, or there were delays in sharing concerns.

From New Labour to the Conservative-Liberal Democrat coalition government

The New Labour government lost the general election in May 2010, and was replaced by a Conservative–Liberal Democrat coalition government. At the beginning of its term in office, the coalition government abolished the £350 million national child database, 'ContactPoint', in which New Labour had heavily invested (Porter, 2010). However, as with previous administrations, *Working together* was subject to a further revision, and a fifth (2010) version replaced previous editions (HM Government, 2010a). As referenced earlier, this fifth edition was some hefty 393 pages long, providing professionals with detailed, prescriptive guidance and attempting to cover every anticipated communicative possibility. In June of the same year, the Secretary of State for Education, Michael Gove, instigated a further review of the child protection system headed by Professor Eileen Munro at the London School of Economics; the final report was published in May 2011, entitled *The Munro review of child protection: Final report – a child-centred system* (Munro, 2011). In addition, as part of the newly elected government's policy of 'transparency', a policy of sharing information with the public about serious case reviews was implemented. During the coalition government's time in office, *Working together* guidance was replaced twice again, in 2013, and, most recently, on 31 March 2015 – not long before the current Conservative government stepped into office (in May 2015).

The 2013 *Working together* guidance (HM Government, 2013) replaced the assessment framework for children in need and their families (DH et al, 2000). Incorporating the linguistic repertoire of the Munro review in taking a 'child-centred' approach, and moving away from 'process', the sixth edition of *Working together* (HM Government, 2013) was significantly reduced in length to 97 pages; its aim was to reduce the bureaucracy in child protection, which was a central criticism in Munro's review of the child protection system. However, most of the procedural guidance and professional responsibilities in the 2013 version remained largely the same as in the previous 2010 guidance. The key message was the same, in that safeguarding children remained everyone's responsibility. To its detriment, however, the guidance ignored research highlighting the inherent complexity in practice, and the significant pressures on services, including overstretched social care duty teams (Broadhurst et al, 2010), and a technical-rational preoccupation with thresholds (White et al, 2015, p 6). This has not been helped by further prescriptive measures imposed on services, such as 'timely' decision making, whereby decisions must be made within certain timescales (Broadhurst et al, 2010). In a similar vein, a seventh edition of *Working together*, published in 2015 (HM Government, 2015a), replaced the 2013 guidance. The number of pages has increased from 97 to 109, and the new version includes a 'myth-busting guide' to dissipate any misunderstandings that might prevent information from being shared in an appropriate and timely manner. Both editions affirm professional responsibility by stating how SCRs have shown that the deaths of children have, in part, been a result of poor information sharing. Notwithstanding the statutory guidance, however, and the emotive messages therein, September 2013 saw the publication of another SCR, this time into the death of four-year-old Daniel Pelka, again highlighting inadequacies in the referral and information-sharing processes.

Born in Poland and migrating to Coventry with his mother and biological father in 2005, Daniel Pelka had two siblings and was the middle child. Daniel suffered prolonged physical abuse, cruelty and neglect at the hands of his mother and step-father. He was pronounced dead on 3 March 2012 as a result of a blow to the right side of his head, which had caused an acute subdural haematoma (a collection of blood on the brain). He was also very malnourished. Daniel's mother, Magdalena Luczak, and step-father, Mariusz Krezoleck, were convicted of Daniel's murder and sentenced to a minimum of 30 years' imprisonment (Coventry LSCB, 2013). The report detailing the circumstances surrounding Daniel's death highlighted issues in the referral process, namely how other professionals often failed to make referrals to children's social care, and in the way referrals were received, rationalised and dealt with by children's social care contrary to the procedural requirements of the referral process outlined in *Working together*. Other issues included the failure of professionals to share general information or take opportunities to address growing concerns about Daniel's welfare. The report commented on communication challenges between different professionals, namely a lack of proactive communication by GPs with other professionals tasked with safeguarding responsibilities. In circumstances similar to those surrounding Peter Connelly's death, the report noted, professionals had made assumptions about the information available to them, and about the actions and views of others, without establishing whether these assumptions were correct. Importantly, between 2011 and 2012, no connection was made between child maltreatment and concerns regarding Daniel's physical injuries, weight loss and lack of growth, so no referral was made to Coventry local authority children's social care services (Coventry LSCB, 2013). However, this was not helped by the hostility Daniel's mother portrayed to professionals. Although the situation was not helped by the hostility shown by Daniel's mother, it was evident that the professionals involved failed to make links between the information they were presented with, and its significance. This raises the issue of professional *sense making* and how available information is (un)connected, interpreted and 'translated' in *context*; these observations, and the complexities therein, are discussed in length in Chapters Six and Seven.

As part of a quality improvement project for addressing issues in multi-agency information sharing, the joint inspection of multi-agency arrangements for the protection of children in England has been rolled out since April 2015. Furthermore, models of multi-agency safeguarding hubs (known as 'MASHs') have proliferated since the coalition's time in office in an effort to prevent children from slipping through the safeguarding net. While there have been some reported benefits of MASH, including facilitating information sharing and improved relationships between professionals, there remain reported barriers to information sharing such as misunderstandings as to what information can or should be shared (Home Office, 2014), although the 2015 *Working together* guidance attempted to address these issues. Such evaluation highlights the fact that information sharing is an aspect of professional work that is not easily sorted. In an attempt to address this issue, the government implemented recommendations from a research project entitled *Information sharing journey: IISAM project*[2] and established a Centre of Excellence for Information Sharing in October 2014. The centre seeks to promote and share good practice with regard to information sharing, including working with local MASHs to identify operational barriers to information sharing, and to find solutions as well as helping to disseminate learning experiences (for further information, visit www.informationsharing.co.uk).

From public inquiries to reforms in child welfare: a summary of what has been learnt

From an examination of key child abuse inquires and reports from the past 40 years, it is evident that persistent problems of inter-professional communication, sharing of information and intervention have haunted professional practice since the 1970s, and are the main problems highlighted in inquiry reports (for example, see Hill, 2003; Munro, 1999; Sinclair and Bullock, 2002; DfES, 2003; Reder and Duncan, 2004; Lachman and Bernard, 2006; Brandon et al, 2008; Ofsted, 2008). Since the Maria Colwell case in 1973, almost all child death inquiries in the United Kingdom have reported failures in effective communication between professionals in the work of safeguarding children (Reder et al, 1993; Falkov, 1996; Brandon et al, 1999; Dale et al, 2002; Sinclair and Bullock, 2002; Laming, 2003). Issues highlighted are the failure to record information, the unavailability or inaccessibility of case files, out-of-date contact details, and a failure by professionals across agencies to make connections between incidents that should have raised concerns about a child (Payne, 2004). Comparable issues have also been identified in the United States (Alfaro, 1988), Canada (Byles, 1985), Australia (NSW Child Death Review Team, 2000) and the Netherlands (Kuijvenhoven and Kortleven, 2010).

A related and reported issue is that of 'communication', namely 'the transfer of information, ideas or feelings' (WHO, 2009, p 16). Traditionally, it was assumed that information could simply be exchanged as long as it was clear, and not affected by 'noise' (White et al, 2015). However, communication is far from straightforward; it involves a 'sender encoding an idea into a message, transmitting that to one or more receivers who then decode it back to the original idea' (WHO, 2009, p 16). Reder and Duncan (2003) suggest that communication (particularly how messages are sent and received) is a complex process, the full extent of which is not wholly appreciated in policy, public inquiries and serious case reviews.

Communication involves a complex interplay between information processing, inter-personal relationships and inter-agency collaboration. The need to communicate purposefully and with meaning to relevant others must be borne in mind by all professionals at all times. Effective communication is the responsibility of both the message initiator and the receiver and, as such, is a mindset and a skill that can be learned, rehearsed and refined. Only then will policies and technological aids have their optimal effect (Reder and Duncan, 2003, p 98).

These authors have suggested that the conclusions of the inquiry teams are limited because they look at failings in very *practical* terms such as not passing information on, or merely making mistakes. Their arguments resonate with earlier claims from Munro (1999), who from an examination of child 'abuse' inquiry reports published in Britain between 1973 and 1994 (45 in total), concluded that there were significant communication errors in 40% of cases. These errors were a result of professionals sometimes hearing others incorrectly, making mistakes in written record keeping and expressing themselves in vague terms that left scope for *misinterpretation*. As such, responses have been rather simplistic, simply rehearsing or restating received advice already on offer to professionals regarding the collection, sharing, classification and storing of information (Parton, 2008). David Howe (1992) comments:

> The analysis of past failings suggested that success in child abuse work would come by: (i) knowing what information to collect about parents in order to determine whether or not they might be a danger to their children; (ii) systematically collecting that information by thoroughly investigating cases; (iii) processing and analysing that information to decide whether or not children were safe in the care of their parents; and (iv) closely monitoring and assessing cases in which children were thought to be at risk. (Howe, 2002, pp 498-9)

Howe's assertion suggests that information has significantly become the crux for safeguarding children, making professionals more accountable, and is an essential commodity in identifying 'high-risk' cases (Parton, 1998). Communication, as a means of professionals sharing information, is talked about within the 'master narrative' (Lynch and Bogen, 1996, p 157) of inquiries, as something that 'just didn't happen' between professions. In this context, 'information' is usually considered to refer to factual message contents, as contained in words spoken or written (Reder and Duncan, 2004, p 95); meanwhile, the interpersonal aspects of communication in information exchanges are also information, but problematically, are often overlooked. In light of the latter, communication is a means by which people relate to one another, and give and receive moment-to-moment signals about themselves, the other person, and the relationship between them. It is also a method in which people signal to others their feelings, experiences, expectations and motivations (Reder and Duncan, 2004). For Pearce (1989), communication is a *social* process because 'individuals interact until they achieve some coordinated way of responding to the world around them, and to each other' (p 84). However, irrespective of such complexities, solutions are largely remedial, simply restating or slightly reworking procedural advice, as seen in the development of *Working together* guidance since its first edition in 1991. Policymakers have assumed that regulating information-sharing procedures is inherently a good thing in reducing human variability; hence a dominant drive towards more detailed procedures has been regarded as a win–win situation. There is an implicit assumption that fault lies with professionals and levels of compliance, rather than the procedure or policy framework or some other factor. However, messages from the Munro review have signalled opposition to such bureaucracy, highlighting that rather than being the remedy for enhancing safe practices it has in fact had contrary effects. Historically, nevertheless, the directives under New Labour echoed in the Colwell inquiry stress professional *responsibility*:

> Improvements to the way information is exchanged within and between agencies are imperative if children are to be adequately safeguarded…. [E]ach agency must accept responsibility for making sure that information passed to another agency is clear and the recipients should query any points of uncertainty. (Laming, 2003, p 9)

Laming referred to an 'imperative' to improve information sharing, making very clear a linear relationship between the passing on of 'clear' information and the work of safeguarding children. In retrospect, examining the subtle shifts and turns in discourses of 'working together', what becomes interesting is the enduring, significant *value* placed on 'information' in the work of safeguarding children and supporting families. In a wider context, the child protection system has entered the 'information society' in which information and communication technologies (ICTs) have increasingly permeated multi-agency child welfare practices (Steyaert and Gould, 1999). Assessments of children and families have become more formalised and decontextualised, with the increased amount of information required ultimately fragmented into 'bits and bytes'. In 2008, Parton observed that information had become a valuable commodity in identifying and managing risk to children (Parton, 2008) as well as in the management of institutional risk (Munro, 2008) by the design of ICS and its 'built-in' micro-management of professional practice. In a critique of ICS, Wastell and White (2014) argue that case records of children's and families' lives have become a central means of achieving accountability by way of providing electronic audit trails for 'evidencing' whether correct procedures have been followed; this is at the expense of professional sense-making processes for understanding complex cases across time and space (p 144). Thus, what has been witnessed over the years in children's services is the implementation of a very sophisticated infrastructure of ICTs such as the ICS, aiming to reduce variability, uncertainty and error in professional performance, while facilitating standardised information-recording and sharing practices. In other words, ICTs such as the ICS have served to promote certain types of information ('designing' particular ways of knowing) while demoting others. However, a number of commentators have argued that the work of safeguarding is actually hindered by the very significant amounts of time that professionals need to service the electronic demands of the 'information machine' (Parton, 2008), at the expense of direct work with children and families.

Parton's prescient observation regarding a paradigm shift from the 'social' to the 'informational' in child welfare work is likely to take some time to overturn. Professionals within children's services have become 'information workers'. Valued in terms of being part of the information chain, the professional role in this context is far from disappearing. The importance of information sharing has been reiterated in the Common Core of Skills and Knowledge for the Children's Workforce as an essential element in delivering more effective services to children, young people, families and carers, with guidance notes stating that sharing information effectively will 'save lives'. Most recently, the establishment of the Centre of Excellence for Information Sharing in October 2014 highlights that information sharing is by no means being removed from the children's safeguarding agenda. Quintessentially then, the rubric of information sharing and saving children's lives has been, and remains, secured.

'Information sharing' in professional practices

Communicating information effectively is considered quintessential for delivering high-quality, safe practices (WHO, 2009). Echoing the findings of inquiry reports into the death of children, research has highlighted that issues in communication are a primary factor in causing patient harm (Leonard et al, 2004). Responding to these failings in very practical terms, healthcare professionals use the structured communication tool SBAR (situation, background, assessment, recommendation), developed by the military (as a high-risk industry), to improve the quality or communication. SBAR includes 'first clarifying the problem, then giving pertinent background information, followed by an assessment of the situation and a recommendation' (WHO, 2009, p 16). It is designed to give 'common' structure to communications between professionals with different styles of communication (WHO, 2009, p 16), and is used in clinical tasks such as handovers of patients, which involve the complex 'intersection between different shifts, units, organizations, professions, ranks, and different professional functions' (Iedema et al, 2009, p 291). International research (including WHO [2008] and the Australian Commission on Safety and Quality in Health Care [2008]) has highlighted major weaknesses in clinical handovers, making this a priority for improving patient care and safety (Iedema et al, 2009). However, as with child welfare, much research in this area has focused on clinicians' compliance with handover structures such as SBAR (Haig et al, 2006) and adherence to checklists (Lingard et al, 2005), leading to 'simplistic and mechanistic handover procedures and guidelines imposed on frontline staff' (Iedema et al, 2009, p 291). In supporting this statement, Iedema et al (2009) continue by suggesting that:

> While such handover solutions may be important for some specialities, and are of particular importance to *inducting* junior staff into appropriate knowledge sharing and information transfer processes, the complexity of clinical work does not permit adherence to these solutions. (p 291, emphasis added)

We can see that both clinical work and social work share similar perils and remedial responses to 'fixing' issues through the standardisation of complex frontline practices. For example, in the quest for improving child welfare information-sharing practices specifically, Richardson and Asthana (2005) observed that from 2002 (to the date of their publication) social workers alone were barraged with (at the very minimum) 16 different guidance documents in relation to multi-agency information sharing and collaborative working practices to support children and families (p 658) One such guidance document was *Guidance on information sharing*, produced by the Children and Young People's Unit in 2003 (Richardson and Asthana, 2005, p 7), with an 'appendix that lists at least 31 separate statutory provisions that should be considered by children's services when sharing information' (Richardson and Asthana, 2006, p 659). In addition, further policy and practice guidance saturated multi-agency practices, including: *Information sharing: A guide for professionals and managers* (DCSF and CLG, 2008); *Information vision statement* (HM Government, 2006b); *Think family* reports (Cabinet Office Social Exclusion Task Force, 2006, 2008); *The Children's plan* (DCFS, 2007); *Embedding information sharing toolkit* (DCSF, 2010); and, most recently, *Information sharing: Advice for practitioners providing safeguarding services to children, young people, parents and carers* (HM Government, 2015) to name but a few.

Whatever their guise, the shared aim of these reports is, and has been, to provide 'good practice' guidance for professionals about sharing information. This is always in procedural terms. Responding always in this way implies that mistakes in passing on information can be remedied, that information is something that can be perfected, and that all that is needed is for professionals or their organisations to get better at doing this. An example of information-sharing guidance is presented as a flowchart in Figure 2.1.

Figure 2.1 offers a framework for professionals and their managers for thinking about the process of information sharing through a structured list of key questions. These are questions that *should* be considered by professionals when they are required or wish to share information; this prompts professionals to think carefully about the legal context.

Perceptively, the presentation of the flowchart leads the eye to believe, somewhat simply, that information sharing is a 'linear' flow of 'facts' from and between agencies. More importantly, professionals are led to believe (with a degree of confidence) that if they behave in prescribed ways (for example, as the flowchart directs), children will be protected from harms, a message profoundly reiterated frequently in public inquiries. Similar to public inquiries, information is presented as an objective phenomenon; while its content may change from case to case or day to day, the implication is that it will be the same kind of object for which this same set of 'rules' (in an informal sense) will apply to all professionals responsible for safeguarding children.

The framework implies that professionals should maintain a sense of balance to ensure that information held by an agency is not exchanged inappropriately (thereby protecting an individual's right to privacy) while ensuring that *enough* information is shared with other 'relevant' agencies to effectively safeguard children. 'Enough' information should be exchanged between professionals on a 'need to know' basis. 'Enough' and 'need to know' are ambiguous terms (recognised by the 'not sure' and 'seek advice' options), but as long as professionals can legitimately account for their decisions and record them, the problem of ambiguity is proposed as resolvable. By laying out reasons as directed in the recording information box towards the bottom of the flowchart, professionals make their judgements objectively available to others for agreement or disagreement, which is a position sought by professionals as the next best thing to certainty.

Figure 2.1: Information sharing: advice for practitioners providing safeguarding services to children, young people, parents and carers

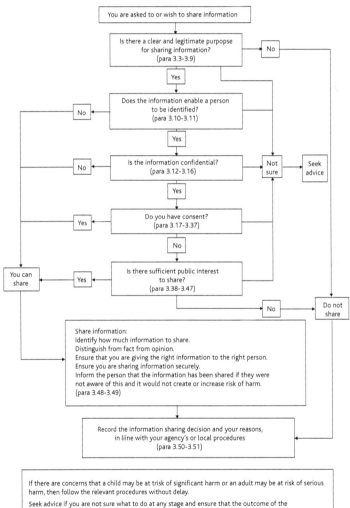

Starting to think critically about information sharing

This chapter's examination of non-accidental child death inquiries has illustrated how information sharing is a continuing and central tenet in effective safeguarding practices, rather than arguably being 'part of' the safeguarding agenda. This is demonstrated very clearly in child welfare policies and guidance literature in which the dominant response to 'information' failures identified in public inquiries has been a rather narrow 'rational-bureaucratic' response (Ferguson, 2007, p 781), which has led to an upsurge of more detailed and complex policy guidance, procedures, legislation about *how* to and *when* to share information.

Practice guidance, for example, as suggested in Figure 2.1, presents information as an 'objective' or finite 'item', with very little sophisticated discussion or problematisation of information's ontology or constitution (properties). In my view, this somewhat disconcerting objectivism rather simplistically suggests that given the right infrastructure and guidance, information-sharing practices across organisational boundaries simply amounts to being well informed and having all the information available, which warrants the passing on of 'facts' by diligent professionals. Indeed, the simplicity of descriptions of 'information' within the policy documents denies the *situated context* of information practices as they happen. Critical commentators foreground 'context' in regard to communication and information exchange (Sarangi and Slembrouck, 1996). Context can refer to the immediate context of this or that conversation, or can refer to background or a broader context of professional and organisational cultures and identities (White and Featherstone, 2005). The permutations of context are far from finite, ranging from the nature of professional relationships and levels of cooperation and trust (Brandon et al, 1999), to formal and informal rules within organisations about behaviour, workload, resources, and/or impact of supervision. Authors such as Goffman foreground the important contextual issue of 'relevance' – in situated contexts certain kinds of knowledge, categories, reasoning processes are relevant and not relevant, influencing the way in which professionals sift, filter and make sense of the social world (Goffman, 1974, 1981). Such frames of reference also shape the type of inter-professional encounter that takes place (that is, phone call, meeting, visit, and so forth, and who is 'permitted' to offer/receive the information). Relevance is also criterial in terms of what knowledge can be gleaned from the encounter, and the action, or series of actions that then follow. This is contrary to the complexities of safeguarding children, which by its very nature requires judgements to be made based on moral and practical imperatives that are all socially organised, and situated, giving rise to practices that are rather more complex than official objectivism implies (Dingwall et al, 1983; Wattam, 1992; Parton, 1997; Taylor and White, 2000).

Destablising officialdom: clear consequences of early categorisation and interpretation

In her examination of child death inquiries, Munro (2005) draws attention to the importance of how information is *used*, particularly with respect to past information that may be easily overlooked. In her earlier work, Munro (1999) claims that child abuse inquiries showed that social workers developed fixed views about cases that were not revised on receipt of new information (pp 748-51). This is compounded by a 'confirmation bias' (Wolfe et al, 1985); there is an overriding tendency to seek information that supports a hypothesis, rather than searching for evidence that does not support the hypothesis (Taylor and White, 2006, p 939). This is particularly seen in the referral process and the early categorisation of cases, as the following extract illustrates:

> Referrals to social services in the borough where Victoria first lived were processed through a one-stop-shop call centre. It was staffed by customer services officers, who decided whether to pass the referral on to the children's social work duty team. They in turn would decide whether the case involved a 'child in need' (with which they continued to work) or 'child protection' (which they transferred on to the investigation and assessment team). A member of the public made a telephone referral, mainly

describing a family in unsuitable accommodation, but also citing a child with a scar on her face, previous evidence of cuts and bruises, who was constantly wetting herself, not attending school, and living in a home surrounded by drug addicts. The referral was logged as a 'child in need' and this premature (mis)labelling of the case led to concerns becoming progressively diluted over multiple message transfers. Social workers eventually visited believing they were dealing with a housing problem. (Laming, cited in White and Featherstone, 2005, p 214)

The dramatic consequence of categorisation is clearly outlined here with regard to the Climbié case, highlighting the sense made of the concerns that the givers of information were articulating. The extract highlights how the referral process provides the context in which all other responses and services are organised, as well as showing the issues of translation and the failure to establish a shared meaning between the parties involved in the information transaction. The Climbié case is no exception in this. In the more recent child death inquiry into the death of four-year-old Hamzah Khan (Bradford Safeguarding Children Board, 2013) we can clearly see the implications of categorisation. In a letter from the MP Edward Timpson, the Parliamentary Under Secretary of State for Children and Families, to Professor Nick Frost, the independent chair of Bradford Safeguarding Children Board on 13 November 2013, the issues of categorisation and the associated concepts of sense making and translation come to the fore. Edward Timpson MP poses the following question to Nick Frost for further investigation:

January 2011 – the school attended by one of Hamzah Khan's siblings in Year 8 reported to children's social care that attendance had fallen to 51 per cent and apparently (it is not clear from the SCR) reported that the child appeared physically neglected. Children's social care decided this was a school attendance issue and declined to assess. Why?

Edward Timpson answers his own question. In this instance, the case had been 'read', translated and subsequently categorised by children's social care as a school attendance issue – the child appearing 'physically neglected' (in the context the information was offered and understood) remained as background 'noise' and offered no signal to suggest possible child maltreatment was made. However, an associated issue of early categorisation of a case such as the ones highlighted, and the 'search' for confirming evidence, is influenced by professional's need to feel certain:

> Social workers like other professionals strive for conditions of certainty. And, at times, they must act as though certainty is easy to come by e.g. when children or adults are perceived to be in great danger. However, we want to press the point that in a great many situations, the 'certain' thing is not necessarily the right thing. To counteract this tendency to make judgements too soon and to look only for evidence that supports the decision, professionals need to stay in uncertainty for longer, and to assess whether, because of the circumstances, there is a need to hold on to doubt whilst taking the time to seek out other possible versions. (Taylor and White, 2006, p 944)

Complexity means professionals having to deal with uncertainty, which is an unescapable feature of professional judgement (Hood, 2014, p 33). As echoed by Taylor and White, it is hard to say with certainty what is 'really' happening in a child's life and whether certain features of the child's life are indicative of child maltreatment, as the phenomenon is socially constructed and based on what is considered normal or morally acceptable (Dingwall et al, 1983). Thus, child maltreatment or child 'abuse' will mean different things to different people in different cultural contexts. In their request for maintaining a position of 'respectful uncertainty' for longer, accepted by Laming in 2003, Taylor and White (2000) further augment their claim that professionals search for information that supports their first hypothesis (or early categorisation of a case), while neglecting evidence that will disconfirm it, an observation similarly made through ethnographies of child protection practice (Wattam, 1992; Parton, 1997). Supporting this argument further, Tetlock (2005) found that experts remained overconfident in their original formulations even after disconfirming evidence had been presented to them. Thus, Munro (2005) notes in her commentary of child abuse inquiries that although there are clear instances where information has not been exchanged between professionals, the issues in fact lie in how information is *interpreted*. Rather than dealing with straightforward, 'certifiable facts' in their day-to-day work, professionals are required to interpret the meaning of what they observe, hear or are told; these meanings are open to a number of interpretations, and therefore interpretation is a task surrounded by ambiguity and uncertainty. It is only after a tragic event such as a child death that what may have appeared ambiguous at the time in hindsight becomes a 'verified concern' that should have been acted on in particular ways. Returning to the Climbié inquiry, a paediatrician highlights an example of interpretative issues with consequential effects: 'I cannot account for the way people interpreted what I said. It was not the way I would have liked it to have been interpreted' (Laming, 2003, p 9).

Here, the intended meaning of the message by the paediatrician was not shared by other professionals' interpretation of the meaning of the information available. By implication, the assumption was that the intended meaning of the information would be understood by other professionals receiving that information in the same way. Supporting this further, clinical handover communication research by Chang and colleagues (2010) suggested that doctors felt that what they were conveying was clear to all those they communicated with – confidence in how well they perceived their communication meant that doctors were less likely to establish whether the intended meaning conveyed was shared by the receiving doctor. Importantly, in a child welfare context, professionals need to interpret received information as a signifier of possible child maltreatment in order to feel that it warrants sharing with other professionals (Munro, 2005). A further issue in interpretation lies in the *translation* process required to make sense of incoming information. This can again be seen in the Climbié case, which highlighted the problems that occur when messages are translated from one medium (for example, direct speech) into another, such as a written form (which is detached from the author, and so interpreted differently):

> Victoria was prematurely discharged from one hospital, having been admitted with suspected non-accidental injuries. Sources of this confusion were multiple, but included a nurse's fax that Victoria was 'fit for discharge' being interpreted by the social worker as meaning the ward staff had no concerns at all. It was intended to convey that, although she was medically fit, social services still had their assessment to undertake (p 148). Then a paediatrician's entry 'discharge' in the medical notes was understood by a nurse to indicate a definite discharge plan. (Reder and Duncan, 2003, p 88)

The sharing of information is not only complex, but also produces different reading and writing contexts (Hall and Slembrouck, 2009) that affect how information is interpreted, as well as the meaning that is attributed to the received information. Again, this was highlighted by White (2009) in respect of Peter Connelly case, with White arguing that issues were not in systemic failings in information sharing but rather in how the information was interpreted. She argues that observing, reporting and receiving information happens in an array of *contexts*, and requires a process of translation in order for the recipient of the information to make sense of it, and to determine whether it is meaningful to a case or not. Thus, a picture emerges that suggests that frequent reports of failings in information sharing are not entirely accurate, and dominant responses to such issues not wholly adequate.

The regulated and much proceduralised measures to encourage information flow and manage risk in children's safeguarding work tell us very little about 'knowledge that guides conduct in everyday life' (Berger and Luckmann, 1966, p 19). Information is inherently social; it is professionals and the public in their organisational and social settings who ultimately decide what information is, what it means, why and when it matters (Brown and Duguid, 2000). Thus in locating a pitch within the 'social' argument, we are left with no alternative but to see the inherent problems in the way information is 'unproblematically' conceptualised in a child welfare, public, media and policy context. Built-on attempts to micro-manage information flows have arguably postponed a drive towards professionals being reflexive about their information practices. The drive to more sophisticated technical-rational solutions, more stringent procedures, legislation and so forth has meant that services (processes) are perhaps 'informationally' overdeveloped, yet somehow information *practices* remain reflexively underdeveloped. Thus, we are prompted to think more broadly and 'outside the box' about how information is constructed by professionals in their various organisational contexts, as well as devising a more critical formula for understanding the how, when and whys of how 'information' is enacted as practice. Importantly, this leaves the question of whether 'information' with a focus on the language of 'sharing' is indeed helpful. I would suggest not. First, we need to ask the question 'What is this thing we call information?', to which we turn in Chapter Two.

Notes

[1] For example, and in date order: *Investigating complex abuse* (HM Government, 2002); *Female genital mutilation* (HM Government, 2003); *Child abuse linked to belief in 'spirit possession'* (HM Government, 2007a); *Safeguarding children who may have been trafficked* (HM Government, 2007b); *Safeguarding children in whom illness is fabricated or induced* (HM Government, 2008a); *Domestic violence, forced marriage and 'honour'-based violence* (HM Government, 2008b); *The right to choose: Multi-agency statutory guidance for dealing with forced marriage* (HM Government, 2008c); *Safeguarding children and young people from sexual exploitation* (HM Government, 2009); *Safeguarding disabled children* (DCSF, 2009); and *Safeguarding children and young people who may be affected by gang activity* (HM Government, 2010b).

[2] See http://informationsharing.org.uk/our-work/resources/information-sharing-journey-iisam-project/

THREE

So, what is this thing we call 'information'?

> What is information?... although the question may appear rhetorical there is a sense in which the answer is that nobody really knows. (Martin, 1995, p 17)

Introduction

Everything around us is potentially information; it affects everything we do. Information is often assumed to mean the same thing to everyone, so there is little discussion about what is actually is, and why and when it matters. Social actors tend to assume that what is information for one person is also information for another. Pollner (1987) argued that we all make a fundamental assumption that we will see the same things, if placed in the same position. In many ways, and in whatever social setting, information 'is what it says on the tin'; any enquiry into its definition would be for a specific purpose, such as the requirement of further delineation for dictionary purposes. However, if we stop and ask what information 'really' means, the answer is more difficult than perhaps first anticipated. Despite the term 'information' being in usage for over 600 years (making an early appearance in one of Chaucer's tales between 1372 and 1386 (Schement and Rubins, 1993, p 177)), this does not make the question any easier to answer – something this chapter's opening quote alludes to.

In this chapter, I do not seek to establish a working definition of what information is, but rather build a critical analysis of 'information' in the context of child protection practice. More specifically, my critical analysis of information sharing is located in the context of 'referrals' as a particular kind of information. In practice terms, understanding referral information remains an important area of enquiry, given the yearly increases in referral figures while resources for protecting vulnerable children steadily diminish. Between 2013 and 2014, 657,800 referrals were received by children's social care services – a 7% increase on the number of referrals received between 2010 and 2011, and an 11% increase on 2012–13 figures (Stevenson, 2015). By drawing on referrals as a particular type of information from a theoretical position, I aim to offer a 'destabilised' picture of information-sharing practices that challenges objectivist policy dictates. While official child welfare documents touch on the issue of relativism, whereby professionals from various agencies have a different language to describe the social world, policy documents still assume that each professional using her or his particular language can elicit 'information' that is finite, stable and, aside from vocabulary, mirrors a social world available to all. As the arguments in this chapter unfold, I will show that this is certainly not the case.

Referrals as a dialect of information sharing

Making a referral is the formal procedure and the official term for passing on information in the context of child welfare and protection. Although information begins life much earlier than at the referral process, in an abundance of informal contexts (the incident prompting the referral, a phone call, a meeting, an email, a word in school, and so forth), it is through the process of making a referral that words and texts are officially deemed information. Referrals are co-produced between professionals and lay individuals at a time when social policy is increasingly consumed by risk, and importantly, the need to protect members of the public from such risks (Beck, 1992). Meanings of risk are spoken into being between individuals within wider contexts, including legal, health and welfare systems (Weedon, 1997, p 105), and predominately act as an idea or 'way of thinking' (Parton, 1996, p 98) – a basis for action, such as sharing information in the form of a referral to children's services. The decision about which children receive support is made against the criteria defined in the relevant child-in-need model (see Appendix 1).

Making a referral involves presenting 'information' in a way that is meaningful to the receiving organisation – for example, children's services – or can at least be reproduced in a way that the recipient can understand. Referrals can be conceptualised as 'translation' devices; putting information into a form that children's social care (systems of communication) can read. From this perspective, kinds of 'hybrid' discourses are created that produce communications that make sense not only to the referring agencies, but also to the agency receiving the referral (King and Piper, 1995). Decisions have to be made on limited, reproduced referral information in terms of its relevance (for example, whether it has been presented to the most appropriate agency), the type of case involved, and the follow-up procedures (Wattam, 1997). The premise of how decisions are made based on the evaluation of referral information is suggested by Platt (2006, p 9) to be as follows:

- the *specificity* (specificity relating to the clarity and detail of the information presented) of harm to a child or children;
- the alleged *severity* of such harm;
- the perceived *risk* of future harm;
- parental accountability;
- the extent of *corroboration* of the referral information.

Similarly, Wattam (1992) identified specificity of information and corroboration, along with motive for referral as key factors in the interpretation of referral information by social workers as receivers of referrals. At the point of referral, professionals are making judgements based on the properties of information, rather than responding to actual harm or injury except in a very few cases (Wattam, 1997). Thus, referral information has a very different function from what it is designed to do.

Referral information is performative; essentially it is information that is designed to perform particular kinds of actions, in the specific (co-produced) occasion of its use, rather than being something that objectively and neutrally reports on particular families, events or problems (such as a child suffering from neglect). The English dictionary definition offered for the verb 'to refer' is 'to hand over for consideration or decision … to direct a client to an agency'. Therefore, implicit in the act of referring is 'another' – an action done on the part of another person. Being the act of 'another', it is by no means surprising that families on the receiving end of professional referrals often feel as if they have been 'shopped' or 'reported' (Broadhurst, 2007); this defines the relationship between families and professionals at the initial referral stage, and more importantly, highlights the ambiguities of what information means at this point to the parties involved. Information changes meaning and action in its co-production between the subject of the referral, the referral maker, and eventually the professional, or agent, receiving the referral. This is because the way in which information is offered and understood, as well as how 'content' is read, is situated or context specific. This can tell us about the disparate realities of professionals and families (in other words, the meaning will not be the same for the family, the professional making the referral or the professional receiving the referral) because of context-specific reasons.

Referral information and indexicality

The philosopher Harold Garfinkel (1967) believed that 'meaning' is always context-specific, or arises in a specific situated context. This has been termed 'indexicality', whereby the meaning of a 'word' is its use rather than the word containing a specific meaning that will always stand *sui generis*. Correct meaning derives from the use of a word in a particular context, where a particular meaning is read (Blair, 2006). In other words, everyday phenomena occur when organisational members 'indexically' use a series of words that become taken for granted over time – words such as 'child protection concerns', 'at risk' of 'significant harm', 'child in need', 'adequate parenting', 'failure to protect', and so forth (Benson and Hughes, 1983). Explained another way, the repetition of an activity, concepts, talk, and dialogue, constructs its own reality to the point where it becomes taken for granted.

Indexicality is an inescapable aspect of communication and poses some troubles for those making and receiving referrals. Although both parties may share the powerful notion that those involved in referral transactions think they are talking about the same thing (for example, child 'abuse'), this belies the issue of context and the fact that readings are always situation-specific. Pollner (1987) refers to this underlying assumption as 'mundane reasoning', that is, an assumption that we all have access (or at the very least the potential to access) to the same underlying reality. However, there are problems that can arise in the translation process. Luhmann's (1995) work is particularly illuminative in understanding some of these problems.

Luhmann's theoretical account of 'autopoietic discourse' suggests that any attempt to blend discourses does not necessarily elucidate new ways of knowing, but rather can create confusion within institutions, as the system of communications (the institution) attempts to translate information into something it can 'hear', something that is not 'noise' (Luhmann, cited in King and Piper, 1995). However, this is not to say that all translations are lost and action leads to nowhere. Rather, it indicates that if the communication cannot be adequately translated ('heard'), confusion and uncertainty can arise. However, the referral, which operates at the boundaries of systems (health, education, social care, criminal justice) works to eliminate this confusion; it is a vehicle for imposing a form of certainty, reducing confusion and ambiguity, clarifying the problem and tracking the 'underlying reality' (Howe, 1996). However, because there are multiple problems that can exist simultaneously in the lives of children and families (as subjects of referrals) and there can be multiple readings of those problems, an issue of 'miscommunication' (Reder and Duncan, 2003, 2004) and 'misinterpretation' (Munro, 1999; White, 2009) between a range of professionals involved in the transaction can quite easily occur. Problems with meaning and understanding are an intrinsic aspect of communication (Reder and Duncan, 2003, 2004; Munro, 2005; White, 2009). Indexicality offers an explanation of the errors that lead to errors in misinterpretation.

Indexicality (that words can have a number of meanings) is on the one hand a useful aspect of communication in that a limited number of descriptive terms can be used in a number and variety of different occasions (Heritage, 1984), but on the other hand, it creates some of the troubles in communication. Thus, 'meaning' always requires a consideration of context (Garfinkel, 1967; Blair, 2006). Context can refer to the immediate context of this or that conversation, or can refer to background or a broader context of professional and organisational cultures and identities (White and Featherstone, 2005). The permutations of context are far from finite. Schutz (1962) also problematises the idea that there is an objective quality to information. Schutz considers information as possessing very diverse meanings for different individuals, based on their own narratives and positions within a social setting – the social setting in which information is encountered contributes to meaning. In addition, Garfinkel (1967) draws attention to the inter-subjective aspect of meaning, in that interpretation is rooted in the situation in which it emerges. Garfinkel suggests that shared meaning is not the same as reaching agreement, but rather it is more about the shared ability to reference linguistic events, such as questions requiring answers (unless rhetorical) or the 'documentary method of interpretation'[1] – taken-for-granted aspects of conversation that allow communication to get done in the first place.

When social scientists talk of 'context' or 'occasion', they are referring to context that extends beyond institutional settings in which talk takes place; they may actually be referring to the placement of a word in a sentence or a sentence in a conversation. In other words, to speak of an utterance as 'occasioned' can be to refer to the position of words in a sequence of utterances or verbal exchange, which, in turn, is part of a broader social and cultural setting (Potter, 1997). Language is therefore not understood in terms of shared semantic representations but rather 'is a result of shared procedures for generating meaning in context' (Edwards, cited in Potter, 1997, p 44). So the question that we should concern ourselves with is not about whether information is right or wrong (its semantic content in relation to its testimony or truths), but rather how information is constructed, how information works as a process, and whether it is doing the job, or the work intended by participants. This gives information a different importance; the concern is not about reflections of 'reality' or a set of 'facts', although this might be the case on certain occasions (for example, where the purpose of the job is to provide a definition, or clarify what is meant). Aligning to this view, information can be regarded as *action* that produces versions of events for the practical purposes at hand. Information presented by a professional referrer, then, reflects that professional's version of an act or occasion, and the context in which it has been offered and understood. Importantly then, 'meanings and understandings of information are not stable or fixed, but are provisional, and situated in the local practices of institutional talk and text' (Taylor and White, 2000, p 77). In other words, it is only when information is constructed in particular ways, in social and organisational settings and contexts that information is deemed meaningful and is regarded and treated as being a particular form of information (such as a referral, an X-ray, a letter, an assessment and so forth; whereas without such setting and context it would just be words and images). These 'products' are informational contexts that are information; context is not a stable description but an outcome of embodied practice (Dourish, 2004, p 29). Dourish (2004) further notes that 'the problem is that context is continually renegotiated and defined in the course of action, and through this negotiation, the actions that individuals undertake can become intelligible and meaningful to each other' (p 29). Thus, the process of making a referral may therefore be considered an informational context.

Information as text

For professional purposes, information is continually reconstructed, reworked, co-produced and represented in various guises or texts. The meaning attributed to a text derives from its context. Referral information is fluid text. What this means is that information may be written material presented on forms, documents, emails, faxes, case files and so on, although it can also mean conversation or talk 'analysed as a piece of language that can be examined for its internal order and how words are pieced together to achieve a particular effect' (Taylor and White, 2000, p 26). In other words, information may be broken down to mean an utterance, something seen, something spoken, something relayed over the telephone or electronically through information and communication technologies (ICTs) such as email, something written, something constructed (on a form) or something that is discussed in an office and so on. These provide different reading and writing contexts that alter the meaning that is attributed to what is being conveyed (Hall and Slembrouck, 2009). In written text where no interaction takes place between the referrer and the receiver of the referral, the reader of the referral imposes his or her meaning on the text.

Referrals are texts that are metaphorically 'co-laboratories' of action. This is a useful metaphor in understanding the referral process, insofar as referrals are a space for professionals to 'test out' hypotheses such as 'is this or isn't this child "abuse"' (Sheppard, 1998). Those who (in)validate child 'abuse' hypotheses are social workers in children's services. Referrals are also a temporal space in which inter-agency professionals request or negotiate some form of action according to normative codes and expectations. All these are interconnected and entangled in what the philosopher Derrida (1981) would term as an 'infinite web of meaning'. Professional referral makers do not only present a version or an account of acts or utterances, but also locate or reflect the presence of them in that text, which will include their inter-personal and organisational needs. Importantly, information cannot be separated from the author of the text and the context in which it is produced. In other words, within the text, referrers are telling something about themselves, and their interaction with the referral process (context) they are engaged with.

Information relating to events that have taken place within families are constructed, and a reality of these families' lives 'designed' as a case for children's services to deal with in order to satisfy the procedural requirements of the referral process, and the perceived functions of the receiving agency – that is, children's social care. Information is about *how* things are made to happen, rather than what information is exchanged (Austin, 1962). This is not to say that referrers necessarily strategically plan information to perform particular actions in every situation, but rather, as the philosopher Gilbert Ryle suggests, it is 'know-how': '...[a]

practical skill and design element that doesn't necessarily imply strategic or well thought out planning' (Ryle, 1949, cited in Potter, 1997). As Derrida (1981) would have argued, this is achieved through 'iteration' – that is, how professionals draw on words and phrases that are used and heard repeatedly in the context of child protection and assume a taken-for-granted quality. Information is therefore by no means independent, but rather 'a product of design'; it is constructed on the basis of a set of theoretical assumptions and decisions (Potter, 1997) using particular 'tools of the trade' (Pithouse, 1998).

Information 'design' using organisational 'tools of the trade'

Referrals and categories of 'abuse' such as neglect can be regarded as boundary objects. Boundary objects are 'documents, artefacts, terms, concepts and forms of reification around which communities of practice can organise their interconnections' (Wenger, 1998, p 105). In offering a conceptual understanding of boundary objects, Bowker and Star (1999) comment:

> Boundary objects are those objects that both inhabit several communities of practice and satisfy the informational requirements of each of them. Boundary objects are thus both plastic enough to adapt to local needs and constraints of the several parties employing them, yet, robust enough to maintain a common identity across sites. They are weakly structured in common use and become strongly structured in individual-site use. These objects may be abstract or concrete. Star and Griesemer (1989) first noticed the phenomenon in studying a museum, where the specimens of dead birds had very different meaning to amateur bird watchers and professional biologists, but 'the same' bird was used by each group. Such objects have different meaning in different social worlds but their structure is common enough to more than one world to make them recognizable, a means of translation.

The creation and management of boundary objects is a key process in developing and maintaining coherence across intersecting communities. (Bowker and Star, 1999, cited in Lee, 2007, pp 309-10)

Boundary objects are therefore created when professionals from different organisations (communities of practice) work together (Bowker and Star, 1999, cited in Lee, 2007, pp 309-10). Boundary objects rely on a standardised structure and can be seen in the way of multi-agency documents or forms (Lee, 2007). An organisation's forms, documents and information processes are 'tools of the trade' to describe the work that organisations do and how they are organised. They create 'background expectancies' (Taylor and White, 200, p 143) of particular practices that are often taken for granted. More importantly, they construct what information is in precise ways. Taylor and White (2000, p 144) suggest that forms and documents may be regarded as 'time travellers' in that they transfer information from one space (such as an organisation, office, telephone conversation and so forth) or time, into another. Information that is presented through organisational texts such as reports, referral forms, or any other document is not 'a neutral undertaking, but one in which social, economic, political, and a variety of taken for granted assumptions are entrenched in the helping relation' (Campbell and Gregor, 2002, p 34). Constructing information using forms and other organisational documents tells us about how the work of agencies is organised; referral information (the foundational basis on which children and family's needs are identified and the actions that are required to meet those needs are coordinated) is as much to do with organisation of work, the nature and form of professionals' knowledge, as it is to do with the needs of those who are the subject of the referral (that is, a child's family).

Artefacts of people and events are created by documents such as referral forms, which make information appear as though it has an underlying reality (for example, 'abuse'), although, as has already been clearly stated, this is not always the case Text within referral forms may act as a signifier for child harm, but on the basis of two decades of research does not do so on most occasions (DH, 1995). Considered in terms of boundary objects, referral forms do not ensure shared understanding, despite supposedly satisfying the information requirements of different communities of practice. In a further discussion of boundary objects from ethnographic work of engineers and assemblers involved in the production and manufacturing of semiconductor equipment, Bechky (1999) makes the claim that:

> The occupational communities negotiated a shared understanding through the use of boundary objects, but they were not always enough. Boundary objects can fail to serve as a translation tool when they are not plastic or flexible enough to be used by all groups. Because the groups had different experiences with the objects and spoke different languages, misunderstanding resulted. These misunderstandings were resolved through verbal translation into the language of drawings, or by the offer of tangible definition, which provided the context needed for shared understanding. (Bechky, cited in Lee, 2007, p 311)

Without the context in which boundary objects are created, errors in translation occur. In a child welfare context, we may question what it is about referrals being received that might help distinguish between those that are signifiers of harm and those that are not. In practice, social workers and other professionals alike have their own ways of determining between signifiers of harm, and those that do not suggest harm (for a fuller explanation, see Chapters Six, Seven and Eight).

In various ways, forms and documents are vessels used to describe and categorise people coming to the attention of child protection services (Gubrium et al, 1989). The structure of the referral form promotes certain ways of knowing, sharing information and reporting concerns. Fragmented into 'bits' and 'bytes', the referrer is forced to present information about children's and families' lives within a certain structure and format. The referral process, as a method of sharing information through a specific textual form, defines what information is at that point. Forms, documents, processes, procedures and targets define the parameters or boundaries of information. The process of referral defines the boundaries of relevance and a form of information from its initiation. As with forms and documents, other components such as performance indicators, procedures and timescales also provide boundaries of information. In other words, these mechanisms 'box off', or define, where information starts and stops, and also serve to reify information as a particular artefact (a referral). Arbitrary timescales, procedures and so forth used to protect children from harm help to define the normative parameters of information (for example, what constitutes a referral or a contact). Through such parameters, information becomes ordered and micro-managed, which hampers the potential fluidity of what is out there to be known about children's and families' lives. Such regulatory efforts 'standardise' the kind of information that is acquired and communicated between professionals and from children and families, thus creating normative boundaries of what referral information is, and when it stops being so and becoming another kind of information, and part of another process.

Normative boundaries of referral information are formed when information at the point of entry into local authority children's services is accepted as 'morally conceivable and believable' (Taylor and White, 2000, p 11). Those who are allowed to have information accepted in this context are those professionals and members of the public who are accepted within child welfare parameters. Referral information invokes different representations of a child and family, influenced by where a professional or member of the public is positioned in relation to information about a child and family, and by the relationship or organisational lens through which the information is projected. In relation to the latter, organisations develop their own 'rationalities' to facilitate decisions on how to act (Teubner, 1983, p 279). However, what may also be important to the receivers of referrals (that is, social workers) is knowing how to locate the organisational or relational relevance of a referrer (May-Chahal and Broadhurst, 2006). Knowing that a referral is from a police officer may be different from knowing that a referral is from a teacher or a health visitor and so forth. Thus, what social workers actually receive as referrals are the positions of referral agents. Although social workers often know referrers, they are still members of the public, teachers or health visitors defined by their (non)organisational 'hat'. Recognition of this diversity of discourses is relevant to the past calls for a 'common language' (Warren House Group Dartington Social Research Unit, 2004) as if a 'common language' would solve the problem (which, crudely put, is 'Do you see it as I see it?'). However, a common language is neither a common context, nor a common action or positioning (Wetherell et al, 2001), and therefore is far from achievable. Similarly, a 'common language' can result in the use of 'habitualised' and stereotyped phrases with little 'diagnostic' meaning (White et al, 2009), resulting in a lack of professional reflexivity and reflectivity.

Information as 'foreign' currency: 'transactions' and the 'value' of information

So far in this chapter what has been described is 'transactions' of information between referral makers and social workers as the receivers of referrals. Understanding information as metaphorical 'currency' that is transacted within and across organisational boundaries is not only a new conceptualisation within child welfare literature, but a helpful one. Deriving from the 'knowledge-based economy', such theoretical insight can be made applicable in practice terms, as the following section demonstrates.

Child welfare information can be conceptualised as both a 'product' or a 'currency' owned by agencies, which can be 'received' and 'donated' for a valued return (Neet et al, 1998). More specifically, we may regard information as 'foreign currency' when we consider difficulties in translation and the (mis)interpretation of information meanings, as I discussed in Chapter Two. In practical terms, value might be considered by professionals in terms of what information is worth (after translation) in respect of making a case in child protection. At and beyond the stage of referral, information transactions can be considered as analogous to a market system (Neet et al, 1998). Information as a metaphorical currency has many 'notes' or forms (phone calls, referral forms, emails, faxes and so forth) and is entrenched and produced through social, economic and political contexts. The value of information exchanged will ultimately depend on the context of the transaction. The child welfare context may be thought of as a 'charitable' marketplace; information is a currency, in which there are 'receivers', and there are 'givers' or 'donators' who participate in related transactions during the 'everyday' business of their work. The role of brokerage and value are important in these transactions.

As information 'receivers', professionals may seek information in an attempt to reach a point of clarity or understanding (Neet et al, 1998) for cases that may appear ambiguous, if that is the required purpose at the time. Information for 'receivers' has value, as it assists in tackling a task more effectively (for example, making more informed decisions about a child or family). During the initial point of contact where children's social care services receive information about a child and their family, the 'receiving' of information is somewhat necessary (as in a charity shop, receivers will be prepared to take anything that comes their way in order to sift through it later), particularly if there is uncertainty and ambiguity about the meaning of the information that is received. Arbitrary timescales, such as initial response teams responding to referrals within one working day of the referral being received, makes the receiving of information crucial, and lend a value to information that would alter under different timescales.

In terms of the referral process, those professionals who are 'donating' information to children's services will often be professionals who have made the referral, or other professionals who know the child or family and who have a potential reason to 'invest' either in the child, or in their own professional position. However, it is likely that only children's social care workers will be 'brokers' of information – that is, the representatives in the information market who act as 'coordinators' between the receivers and donators of information; they decide on value. Furthermore, they are the service that will choose to 'invest' in particular kinds of information, and 'bank' that information for a later date (for example, storing information on ICT systems until such time as it becomes of value). The role in brokering is complex; it requires social workers to facilitate translation and coordination between communities of practice, and reach negotiated meaning between various perspectives (Wenger, 1998, p 108). At the referral stage, social workers are legitimised professionals tasked with evaluating the information they receive (for example, whether a case does or doesn't constitute child maltreatment, and whether it is something that requires immediate attention).

The value placed on information is reflected by the response given to that information. Information with 'low value' would be information that has no meaning for the agency or is something that is 'not for us' to deal with. Information that is 'not for us' can cover a multitude of options such as 'not for us now' (bank it), 'not enough for us at the moment' (hold until confirmed) and likely to receive 'no further action', with the transaction terminated at the point of entry into the service. On the other hand, information with 'high value' (information about a child and family that meets the threshold for receiving a service) will receive a service, and thus the transaction will continue to the next stage. For information transactions to take place, each party (agent or member of the public) will have specific kinds of information because of where they are positioned in relation to information, and also what is considered 'relevant' to generate receiving and donating transactions. Informational transactions rely on the value assigned to participating in that transaction. Receivers and donators have to believe that a transaction is worth making, or that they will benefit in some way. These transactions also rely on 'know who'; that is information about 'who knows what' and 'who knows how, and what to do' (Foray and Lundvall, 1996, p 116).

Considering information as a 'currency', with varying value denominations operating within organisational 'marketplaces', conceptualises information-sharing activity very differently from policy dictates, although in practice, different levels of value placed on received and donated information will, I am sure, resonate with professionals within their respective organisations. In practice terms, value may be inter-personal, organisational or both: seen in terms of its significance or relevance to a case, the emotional value for the referrer (a feeling or hunch that something isn't right), a means of reducing professional anxiety (what could happen if I don't pass this on), reciprocity (getting something back) and more besides. Information, then, is not arbitrary or of neutral value. It is by understanding information in terms of its value that has the potential to improve how information is shared, received, rationalised and dealt with across various organisational contexts.

Conclusion

Professional information and the work that is done with it are important instruments for safeguarding children. There are particular kinds of information that characterise the social work profession and the nature of its knowledge base. The identity of social workers, which is negotiated through literature and training, constructs the social worker as an 'information worker' (Parton, 2008) who uses profession-specific literature as the basis for her/his work. The same will also be true of other professionals.

Information that is 'transacted' between professionals is a product of ever more coercive design rather than something that occurs naturally. The act of sharing information is a reciprocal behaviour that derives sequences of action in changing sets of circumstances; interpretation is inherent in this task. Information that is exchanged across interdisciplinary boundaries has to be made compatible with the context in which it is generated and received. So, for example, information that is generated in an educational environment has to be designed to fit the normal expectations that the receiving agency (that is, children's services) is used to, identifies as being part of its business and feels able to deal with.

Information is also performative; it can be broken down into a series of actions that have a multitude of meanings. As such, the process of making a referral can be a method of passing on a problem; a mechanism that provides a level of reassurance for the professional referrer; a process that fulfils professional obligations or expectations; a request for a service or a cry for help; and more besides. Response services are currently not explicitly organised to explore and respond to these 'performances'. Traditionally, policy guidance and documents inform professionals about ways in which information sharing should be operationalised; these continue to treat the process as only a method of passing on a possible underlying reality of unmet need, but, as this chapter has shown, this is certainly not the case. In many instances, making a referral to children's social care is an option for the meeting of public or professional needs and therefore the referral route may not be the appropriate course of action where an alternative would be better suited. Breaking information down into a series of performative actions with varying levels of value and meaning may facilitate greater understanding of multi-agency professional's needs and information-related behaviours, an area explored in greater detail in the next chapter.

Managers' questions for reflection

1. How might children's services organise their responses differently when receiving, rationalising and responding to referrals?
2. What contexts can be created at point of contact in children's social care to distinguish between public and professional needs and protecting children from harm to ensure that the referral route is utilised most effectively?

Professional questions for reflection

1. What strategies do you (social workers) use to filter out referrals? What factors influence the way in which you rationalise and respond to referrals?
2. What factors do you (as a referrer) filter into your referral so that it is picked up by children's social care?
3. Do you consider the 'value' of information you give or receive? Does this affect what you do with information?
4. What would you consider to be 'high-value' information? What makes it high value? What would you do with this type of information, and why?
5. Are there ever times when referral information is not consistent with what you go out and see? How do you resolve this disparity?

Note

[1] This refers to the way that words and collections of words stand for a whole range of things; it is indexical and dependent on context. Without the documentary method of interpretation, conversations would be endless (we would have to explain what is meant by every phrase and word).

FOUR

Understanding professional information need and behaviours

Introduction

The previous chapter considered 'information' and 'information sharing' through a philosophical lens in the context of referral making and taking in child protection. A 'destabilised' picture of 'information sharing' has already begun to unfold, and challenges received ideas that 'information sharing' is merely an institutional safeguarding task, involving diligent professionals being well informed, having all the information available and passing on 'facts'. Although this may indeed be the case on certain occasions, it is certainly not the case all of the time. The stock vocabulary of 'information sharing' is partially responsible for producing this picture – a picture that fails to accent the complexities of what information means and why and when it matters to professionals in their respective everyday work of protecting children. Eileen Munro (2005) critiques the use of the term 'information sharing', suggesting that it serves to 'gloss', or disguise, a range of interrelated tasks that are subsumed under the information-sharing umbrella. Furthermore, the term condenses and simplifies a range of complex information-related behaviours that reflect professional information needs that arise in context. In order to understand the latter, and to throw some light on to those issues of information-sharing in child protection work highlighted repeatedly in public inquiries and serious case reviews, we are forced to look further afield to the discipline of 'information science' (also known as 'human information behaviour', Wilson, 2006). You might say this is another piece of the jigsaw, in trying to build up a complete picture of the complexity of information practices across a multi-agency, child welfare spectrum.

Using flowcharts to understand 'information sharing' and 'information behaviour'

Diagrams are a good way of visualising and thinking through problems. Take, for example, the information-sharing flowchart presented in Chapter Two, and aimed at professionals with responsibility for safeguarding children. This flowchart is part of a 'tool kit' that provides busy professionals with an economical 'how to guide' about when and how, to share information. The flowchart is one of many 'simplificatory devices' (Law and Mol, 2002, p 2) that provides 'easy to follow' steps that professionals can digest, understand and feel they can work with, irrespective of the uncertainties that surround day-to-day practices. In other words, the information-sharing flowchart helps professionals to understand, in a manageable form, how they are 'officially' expected to perform an institutional task most effectively. Such diagrams are, however, reductive in their design in that they order, divide, simplify and exclude (Bauman, 1989), arguably to the point where they are unsympathetic to the muddier waters or situational contexts in which professionals may find themselves in day-to-day practice. Nevertheless, the functionality of their design is valuable in terms of thinking about a concept, and this can help us to understand professional information behaviour.

Using the discipline of information science, Wilson (1981) devised a framework for thinking about information behaviour, and describing information-seeking activity, on the part of an information user, as shown in Figure 4.1.

Drawing on the concept of 'information behaviour', complexity is introduced into explanation as a source of a variety of information needs that can influence generalised information behaviours. While 'purpose' is considered central to the information-sharing flowchart contained in government guidance advice (HM Government, 2015a, p 12), Wilson's model foregrounds the importance of 'need'. Wilson's flowchart

Figure 4.1: Wilson's original model of information behaviour (1981)

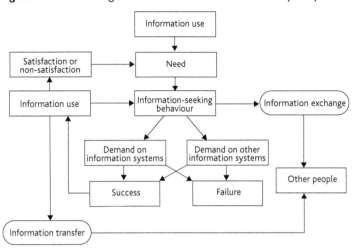

infers that a series of activities relating to information-seeking behaviour occur as a result of the needs of information users. Information need is defined as:

> [a] subjective experience that occurs only in the mind of the person in need and, consequently is not directly accessible to the observer. The experience of need can only be discovered by deduction from behaviour or through the reports of the person in need. (Wilson, 1981, p 552)

While this statement appears to reflect a somewhat objectivist, behaviourist stance, Wilson's notion of information need may have application in an intersubjective-constructionist position. It is proposed that for any need to be satisfied, the information user will make demands on either formal or informal sources or services; the outcome will be either successful (an individual will use the information, and their identified need is, or is partially, met) or will result in failure (in that the person feels their need has not been satisfied and therefore begins the process again). Important in the model is the illustration of other people involved in the process (likened to that of 'information sharing', which Wilson terms 'information transfer'), and, as such, information-seeking behaviour may include other people, through channels of information exchange, to satisfy a user's need. Through this process, information that is valued as useful (which can be understood as inter-subjectively co-produced as useful) may be exchanged between people for their respective co-produced uses.

Wilson recognises 'need' as a 'subjective' construct, which in child protection terms is not easy to legislate for and therefore is not recognised in government information-sharing guidance in the same way as Wilson describes. In government guidance, 'need' is perhaps implied in terms of organisational need, and is not articulated explicitly as either an inter-subjective or personal 'need', as can be inferred by Wilson's diagrammatic illustration. Rather, 'need' is described in child welfare policy in organisational terms, such as legal requirements, procedure (that is, what to do) and so forth, which give the demeanour of authority and certainty. This, however, only reflects part of the picture. Organisational needs are largely bureaucratic – they are 'legitimate' needs that are authorised to be shared; they are defined by the functions of organisations and the roles of professionals that represent them. Organisational needs are not clouded by any form of smoke screen by virtue of such legitimacy. However, also relevant are individuals' professional needs, which arise in various contexts within an organisational setting; these cannot be legislated for in the same way as organisational needs despite their importance. Arising professional needs may be characterised as uncertain and inter-subjective compared with their organisational counterpart; the two types of need often exist in parallel but professional needs largely remain from view.

Uncertainty and information-seeking behaviour

Protecting children is characterised by uncertainty and is intrinsically tentative (Parton, 1998; Taylor and White, 2006). Child welfare professionals are required to make decisions in the context of the complex and often shifting needs presented by children and families. The uncertain and unpredictable nature of family life means that making sense of information is complex; making sense of a child and family's world is surrounded by ambiguity, and co-produced meanings (from various sources of information) can be fleeting and unstable. Despite the uncertain terrain of child welfare work, the pursuit of certainty has been an enduring endeavour on the part of policymakers and professionals alike. Rather than being merely a mandated institutional task, information-seeking behaviour (as part of the process of information sharing) on the part of frontline workers is perhaps a means by which the need to feel certain can be fulfilled. In aligning to this view, Newcomb (1953) observed that 'we are more likely to find increased communication activity in the form of information seeking, giving and exchange under conditions of uncertainty and disequilibrium' (Wilson, 1999, p 265). Similarly, in a more recent reflection in a healthcare context, it is concluded that:

> Uncertainty exists when details of situations are ambiguous, complex, unpredictable, or probabilistic; when information is unavailable or inconsistent; and when people feel insecure in their own state of knowledge or the state of knowledge in general. (Brashers, 2001, p 478)

Here, Brashers ascribes 'details of situations' and 'inconsistent information' with insecurity. Brashers (2001) further suggests that an 'ideology of uncertainty reduction' permeates healthcare practices, which often yields a negative emotional response such as anxiety or fear (p 487). The issue of uncertainty is perhaps even more heightened in childcare social work than in healthcare, given that childcare professionals operate in a context of error and blame (Parton, 1998; Broadhurst et al, 2009). Attempts to reduce, rather than manage, uncertainty have increasingly become a dominant feature of child protection as a result of negative and damming reports by the media in response to public child death inquiries – reports that typically highlight what social workers have failed to do in such cases. Practitioners may well wish to consider at this point whether their own information behaviours alter in cases surrounded by ambiguity and uncertainty, and what information needs arise as a result of this.

Wilson (1999) suggests that uncertainty emerges as a result of a perceived problem in an individual's social world, which, in the words of Schutz and Luckman (1974), leads to a discrepancy between typifications assigned to the world, and a phenomenon that does not in the first instance, fit with what is already known from similar observations (typifications of the world). This creates problems that require uncertainty resolution. Wilson (1999) suggests that resolution requires a process in which individuals identify a problem (What kind of problem is this?) and seek to define the problem (What is the nature of the problem?) in pursuit of reaching the final stage of establishing how the problem can be dealt with and resolved (p 266). Krikelas (1983) assigned 'information gathering' and 'information giving' as significant factors in information-seeking behaviour, and again foregrounds issues of uncertainty as influencing such behaviour:

> Imagine a situation in which a person becomes aware of a state of uncertainty about a problem (question, issue) and attempts to reduce that state of uncertainty to an acceptable level. The cause of that uncertainty may be a specific event or simply an ongoing process associated with work, ordinary life or both … only a small part of a person's ongoing needs would produce an outward behaviour that we might identify as information seeking. Furthermore, the level of 'urgency' and the perceived importance of the problem … would influence the pattern of information seeking. (Krikelas, cited in Case, 2004, p 119)

Krikelas highlights the notion of 'needs' as, in part, creating a behaviour that may be observably recognised as information seeking. He suggests that information gathering is a result of a perceived need, in which uncertainty is created by an event. He further explains that some needs can be placed on hold (or 'banked' for later), while others require immediate attention depending on the urgency that is assigned to a situation. In meeting an information need, Krikelas proposes that an information user will select a source or channel that is identified as being most appropriate to meet the user's perceived need. In taking this idea further, Johnson (1997) introduces the concept of the 'social network' of the information user, asking the question of who can answer any questions, or meet the individual's need, or know how to find out how to do so. This resonates with social work practice all too clearly, but I think these suggestions could be extended even further still; what motivates professionals to seek information in various contexts in the first place? I shall offer one explanation of this using my own reflections as a social worker in practice.

Intuitive practice, risk and uncertainty: the motivation for information-seeking behaviour

Case scenario

Child B was the victim of serious physical abuse at the hands of his step-father, Mr R. Mr R was convicted of the physical abuse of his step-son and has not been permitted to have any contact with Child B, and therefore not permitted to enter the family home in which Child B, his mother and Mr R's biological children reside. Mr R has informal contact with his wife and biological children outside of the family home. Mrs R's wish is for Mr R to return to the family home. Mr R has presented to many professionals involved in the child protection process as being 'aggressive', resentful and mistrusting of *all* professionals and their involvement. A risk assessment was carried out to establish first, the level of risk Mr R still posed to Child B, and second, the mother's ability to ensure the safety of her son in respect of her husband. Child B has said on each visit that he "wants his dad to come home". Mrs R, her husband and Child B have been visited on a number of occasions in various locations (school, home, social services meeting room) to enable professionals to gather information forming the basis of the risk assessment, and any subsequent decisions to be made.

Context: a home visit

I visited Mrs R at home while Child B was at school. Mrs R had forgotten about my visit and presented as anxious. The nature of the visit was to discuss the progress of the risk assessment, the predicted timescale for its completion and emerging concerns to date. While talking to Mrs R downstairs, I had a strong sense that Mr R was upstairs, and therefore asked Mrs R if I could use the bathroom. Mrs R hesitantly agreed and followed me upstairs carrying two younger children in her arms and waited for me to come out. She was talking very loudly, appearing to 'alert' someone to the fact that I was upstairs. All bedroom doors were shut, the children's bedroom doors having locks on the outside, which was a further concern. Based on Mrs R's anxious behaviour throughout the visit, I felt that Mr R was in one of those rooms. Despite my feelings, I became 'paralysed' about asking Mrs R to open the doors. The 'not knowing' of what I would do if Mr R was in the house, and further the possible risk Mr R posed to me as a social worker 'finding' him somewhere he shouldn't be, created an overwhelming sense of anxiety; the uncertainty about how Mr R would react, and the fact that my phone was downstairs, exacerbated this feeling. My feelings of anxiety meant that I left the visit without the evidence needed to resolve the uncertainty of the situation.

Motivation and information-seeking behaviour
I returned to the social work office unsettled by this uncertainty, unsure about whether my feeling was accurate as I had no evidence to prove anything. Motivated by the need to discuss my (in)validated findings with a fellow professional, I identified the health visitor allocated to the family as the most appropriate person. She knew the family well and her role in the child protection process meant that she would have the relevant information to meet my need and inform my assessment of risk. The health visitor 'confirmed' that she also felt that Mr R had been visiting the house. She stated that she and colleagues had increased the number of unannounced visits they made in the hope of 'catching him out' and gathering the evidence needed, but that Mr R was 'too clever'. I later spoke to the school nurse, who confirmed that she had spotted Mr R close to the house at 7.30 am on a number of occasions when he had "no business of being there". Despite a 'network of feelings' with regard to Mr R being at the family home, there remains no evidence for substantiation, and therefore the case is considered one for closing. Nevertheless, the information was recorded ('banked for later') and a request made for more announced home visits in an attempt to seek out the information needed as evidence of these concerns.

Illustrated here is that motivation is a key driver for professional information-related behaviours such as information seeking that is prompted by feelings, uncertainty and risk. However, Johnson

(1997) proposes *salience* as a significant motivator in determining whether information is sought. Salience in this context means that information is not only perceived as being *relevant* to an individual's need, but also *appropriate*. Salience of information can be used to solve a problem, bridge a gap between what is and what is not known, and also to resolve ambiguity (Dervin, 1992), as my own reflections of practice imply. It is important to explore the underlying reasons why professionals share information when it is not entirely obvious why they have done so (in other words, why is that information relevant?). Already it is becoming apparent that there is more than just a moral and legal duty to sharing information, as authors such as Johnson and Dervin imply. However, in child protection practices, little is understood about individual motivations for seeking or sharing information. In providing an explanation, Wilson (2006, p 682) introduces the notion of 'stress' as an area for further consideration, in that it may explain 'why some people engage in information seeking, and others do not, but it is apparent that, in the same situation, and under the same apparent "stress", some people will seek information to help them alleviate that stress and others will not' (Wilson, 2006, p 682).

Apart from feelings of stress, motivations of child welfare professionals experiencing other affective states, such as fear, anxiety and so forth, in various contexts may also be worthy of further exploration. There is currently no system for understanding this. Norman (2004) argues that experience of everyday events is conditioned not solely by practical or 'logical' concerns, but also fundamentally by aesthetic and emotional ones; by virtue of child protection work, Norman's assertion is highly plausible. Johnson (1997) concluded that motivation for information seeking results from an individual's role within social systems rather than being the basis of resolving a perceived problem.

Information as social practice: context and place

Johnson (1997) highlights the importance of *context* in sense making, and further that information-seeking behaviour is context-specific, and should be understood in this way, although this is by no means a straightforward concept. In child protection work, critical commentators foreground 'context' with regard to communication and information exchange (Sarangi and Slembrouck, 1996), discussed in detail in Chapter Two.

Information-sharing and information-seeking activity become shaped, and are social practices that occur in various 'communities of justification' (Rorty, 1979) through negotiation. Sundin and Johannisson (2005) define a social practice as 'an institutionalized activity that consists of more or less formal sets of rules concerning among other things, what should be considered 'proper' information seeking' (p 112). Here, 'institutionalised' refers to socially agreed ways of acting, rather than any specific institution per se. What is considered 'proper' information sharing is something subject to social agreement, rather than any formal organisational advice or guidance. Understanding information in this way aptly illustrates the contingent nature of the social; that is, the potential for individuals or agencies to influence how information is shaped, and how, why and when it matters. Furthermore, it allows information to be considered in terms of an instrument for the negotiation of rules that apply within various communities of *justification* rather than information being something that is transacted between people, or through mediums such as information and communication technologies (Sundin and Johannisson, 2005). Considered in this way, information is an instrument for action and not something that is waiting to be revealed. Information is generated and legitimated within and across different contexts (or as Rorty [1979] would term communities of justification) producing a variety of meanings.

Understanding information behaviour in context sees a conceptual shift in traditional understandings of information sharing by considering the reasons why people might engage in such behaviour in the first place. Fisher and Naumer (2006) have taken this further by examining work on 'information grounds' that are said to facilitate information sharing in both spontaneous and prescribed ways; here they introduce the notion of 'place', which they argue is an inherent aspect of context. The notion of 'place' here is articulated in 'which everyday happenings occur with some predictability' and 'allows for the presence of other legitimized others'. In this way, 'people who share physical and conceptual space are within a common landscape of cultural meaning' (Fisher and Naumer, 2006, p 96), which can be seen, for example, in a case conference, core group, strategy meeting and so forth. Chatman (2000) further notes:

> Within the conceptualised understanding of information behaviors, the legitimized others place narrow boundaries around the possibilities of those behaviors. In other words, legitimized others shape, change, or modify the information that enters a small world in light of a world view. In this instance, a world view is that collective sense that one has a reasonable hold on everyday reality. (p 3)

Chatman's articulation suggests that background 'expectancies' or normative boundaries regulate the information behaviours of professionals. Fisher and Naumer (2006) suggest that such behaviours are fostered by the 'information grounds' in which they occur. Tuominen and Savolainnen (1997) suggest that information grounds are 'environment[s] temporarily created when people come together for a singular purpose but from whose behaviour emerges a social atmosphere that fosters the spontaneous and serendipitous sharing of information' (1997, p 81). Information grounds as a focus of study emerged inconsequently from Pettigrew (1999) during fieldwork at a community foot clinic. The study found that the place of 'clinic' as a physical and social setting promoted information sharing and particular kinds of information behaviour. Importantly, Pettigrew observed that a person's information needs were rarely revealed in a formal context, but rather featured during informal conversations when individuals shared their situations with others. Such research findings signal that information grounds create organisational boundaries as to what information is, what information is promoted, and also what information becomes 'silenced'. In other words, information grounds can affect whether information is shared or not, an aspect that does not feature in the language of child welfare and protection.

The social organisation of information as text

Texts are central vessels in child protection work. Broadly speaking, texts allow us to understand how information is negotiated and enacted through the actions of others in broader social practices. McKenzie's (2006) ethnographic work examined textually mediated information practices in a midwifery setting. The study sought to explore the relationship between individuals and texts in the 'everyday' of midwifery work. The authors refer to texts primarily as documents that actively construct, and in turn, are constructed by social contexts (McKenzie, 2006, p 74). Furthermore, texts are performative; they are not passive containers of information, but rather may be regarded as metaphorical 'windows' through which observers can 'see' the social organisation of those that use texts, as Dorothy Smith (1990) comments:

> Texts are not seen as inert extra-temporal blobs of meaning, the fixity of which enables the reader to forget the actual back and forth work on the piece or pieces of paper in front of her that constitute the text as a body of meaning existing outside time and all at once…. The text is analysed for its characteristically textual form of participation in social relations. The interest is in the social organization of those relations and penetrating them, discovering them, opening them up from within, through the text. The text enters the laboratory, so to speak, carrying the threads and shreds of the relations it is organized by and organizes. The text before the analyst, then, is not used as a specimen or a sample, but as a means of access, a direct line to the relations it organizes. (pp 3-4)

McKenzie's work as part of discursive practice suggests that practices are socially organised; they mould exchanges of information in various contexts between a variety of professionals, and the individuals who are the subjects of intervention. In other words, information exchange is structured around the record as text, and reflects the structure and work of an organisation.[1] Through text, professionals in their organisational setting mediate between systems and people, in that 'they negotiate the disjuncture between rational, impersonal "ways with words" and embodied personal "ways with words" many times during a workshift' (Stooke, cited in McKenzie, 2006). Campbell and Gregor (2002) note that 'participants in local settings find their actions coordinated by the requirements of working with the text' (p 32), although the meanings attributed will be different for different professionals, in various organisational settings. In relation to referrals as text, they are a vehicle and a facilitator of translation, in which different professionals with different organisational relevancies can share information in a standardised way to children's services that is perceived to be understandable by all, or, as Davies and McKenzie (2004, p 81) note, they act a 'repository housing and coordinating data from other records, and a temporal boundary object, coordinating multiple temporalities as well as multiple communities of practice'.

McKenzie highlights how knowing the author of the text (as an agent of an organisation) is important for providing contextual information. The reader of the text can assign meaning to the text, in that what is presented follows conventions of information behaviour that are to be expected from an individual within that social practice. More importantly, McKenzie highlights that it is this *reading context that shapes a professional's information need*, and the action that then follows. Different reading and writing contexts influence meaning attribution. As seen in the Climbié case, and discussed in Chapter Two, disparate interpretations arise when messages are translated from one medium into another, such as from the spoken to the written word, or vice versa. Although the following passage has already been highlighted in Chapter Two, it warrants reiteration:

> Victoria was prematurely discharged from one hospital, having been admitted with suspected non-accidental injuries. Sources of this confusion were multiple, but included a nurse's fax that Victoria was 'fit for discharge' being interpreted by the social worker as meaning the ward staff had no concerns at

all. It was intended to convey that, although she was medically fit, social services still had their assessment to undertake (p 148). Then a paediatrician's entry 'discharge' in the medical notes was understood by a nurse to indicate a definite discharge plan (p 274). (Reder and Duncan, 2003, p 88)

Emerging as very pertinent here is that different reading contexts produce different relationships to information, and different meanings attributed to information that is received. Thus, contrary to received ideas and policy dictates, issues in communication and information sharing are not easily sorted. Klein (2004) argues that complex problems, such as those that child welfare professionals are faced with in their day-to-day work, cannot necessarily be solved by new information, or by adding new information intermediaries or tools such as ICTs. What we are dealing with are complex (social) systems operating within other complex systems (Byrne, 1998). Such systems have non-linear dynamics, and thus cannot be determined by a finite set of rules (Hood, 2014, p 31). Complicated 'welfare' problems such as resolving issues in communication and information sharing are not reducible to a quick-fix solution, but rather are something that must be continuously managed through reflexive practices (Taylor and White, 2000). The 'new managerialsim' of welfare (Clarke et al, 2000) defies this notion – 'improvement' projects through the implementation of various guises allude to professional compliance, via performance indicators and inspection reports (Hood, 2014). These do not reflect complexity experienced by professionals, who, as a consequence, are likely to implement their own 'street-level' solutions (Lipsky, 1980) to deal with 'the swampy lowlands' of frontline practice (Schon, 1991). In going some way to fulfil this assertion, I now turn to thinking differently in how information is shared between professionals by utilising empirical data detailing the day-to-day of child protection work, highlighting professionals' information behaviour to illustrate the complexity that lies within.

Applying information behaviour theory into child welfare practices

Making a referral operates as an authorised need in the process of making children safe. As discussed in detail in Chapter Three, making a referral also has an unauthorised function in meeting professional information need, having the potential to reduce professional anxiety, pass on accountability, carry out a professional role and so forth. The latter is less visible, but equally, if not more, important. From the interviews carried out during research for this book with professionals frequently making referrals to local authority children's services departments key themes emerged, such as trust, strength of network, how information is exchanged and levels of uncertainty. These appear to influence whether information-seeking behaviour leads to information being utilised in a variety of ways, what motivates this, and ultimately whether professional needs are satisfied. Thus, influenced by Wilson's model of information behaviour in 1996, an adapted version of Wilson's flowchart is presented in Figure 4.2, capturing key themes that not only foreground professional information need, but professional information behaviour more generally, reflecting interview data from professionals.

There are clearly limitations with flowcharts, and these are outlined earlier in this chapter. It is clear that the scope of the findings is much greater than is possible to fully convey in a flowchart, but nonetheless the figure does serve to simply illustrate an alternative understanding of how information practices work on the ground in day-to-day professional work. The problems of linearity are similarly applicable, as noted earlier. However, I would argue that the flowchart presented in Figure 4.2 is being used as a data illustration tool rather than an information-sharing 'how to' guide for professionals in policy guidance, which is the purpose of the flowchart presented in Chapter Two. Rather, Figure 4.2 reflects just one, alternative, understanding of how information practices might be operating in a child welfare context. The flowchart depicts professional information needs of the information user that arise in context (outside of their context, these needs would not arise or hold

Figure 4.2: Flowchart of inter-professional information behaviour adapted from Wilson's (1996) model of information behaviour

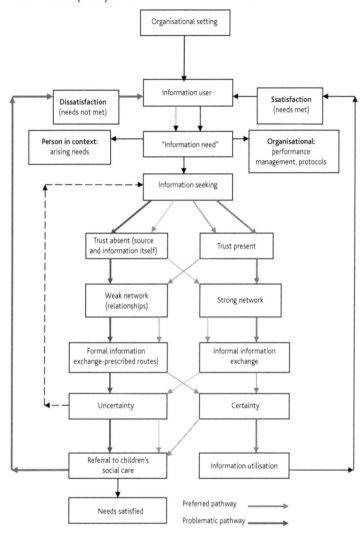

the same meaning), and also ('legitimate') needs as defined by the organisation and their informational requirements. The flowchart highlights features of trust (levels in both source and in the information given), strength of network (based on perceptions of the relationship between the information user and source of information), routes of exchange (whether formal or informal) and levels of certainty following the information-seeking behaviour of the information user. These factors determine whether the information user is satisfied or not that their information needs have been met, whether the information will be used, whether information-seeking behaviour continues if the information user is dissatisfied, or whether a referral to children's social care is required.

The flowchart depicts two pathways: one that is preferred and one that may be considered problematic. The preferred pathway is when there are high levels of trust in the information that is offered, and also levels of trust between the information user and the source giving the information. Levels of trust will be determined by relationships – good relationships between information users and givers will extend beyond a mandated network of professionals tasked with working together, or the formal requirement of bringing people together. When networks are based on voluntary relationships, information exchange takes on a less formal, prescribed level – the added benefit of this is that requests for information do not result in any delay. Via this route, the information user is able to reach a level of certainty in a more timely fashion, which arguably means that the information user is then able to utilise the information they have been given. The information user is left satisfied as their information needs both at an organisational level and in terms of those needs arising in context. The problematic pathway depicts the opposite, in which the information user is often left dissatisfied, and therefore will attempt to satisfy their information needs by way of making a referral to children's social care. However, the response (or not) from social services can determine whether the information user is satisfied (referral responded to/action taken in the way the referral wants) or can lead to dissatisfaction (no response/feedback, or no action taken by social services) in which the information user may continue with information-seeking behaviour in order to satisfy their presenting information needs.

Foregrounding professional need in everyday practice

To illustrate professional need specifically, I now turn to part of an interview with a police officer at a family protection unit, one of the bodies that frequently makes referrals to children's services. The police officer describes what information she needs to do her job. She acknowledges that information needs for her unit team may not be the same for other unit teams within the police station:

> "In terms of our role we only need the family details and the nature of the incident or concern because that's basically what we are dealing with. We are not dealing with long-term work. It might be different for the [sexual exploitation] team because they do long-term work with families. I need to know what has happened in terms of an incident, background of the family, family details, so I can make an initial judgement, because nine times out of 10 we are dealing with an incident that has already happened." (Police officer 1)

Information need is tied to role; the work of the police is to prosecute, as the police officer continues:

> "I think if they are involving a criminal offence against a child then I don't think that can be done any other way because we are the agency for prosecuting criminal offences, so it's perhaps a little different for us." (Police officer 1)

The police officer makes it clear that information that her agency needs is information to aid prosecution. The agency will take any information it is given because it knows it will be tested out through an investigation. However, it passes on information to children's services to see if it can get information back to help with prosecution, for example:

> "I think as a general rule we accept the information that we are given. If a referral comes to me from the referral and assessment team, from the duty team, if they ring me and say 'We've got a child here whose making this allegation', then generally speaking I

would accept that because we know them well. The only research I would do is background on the family to see what we know about them to assist in the investigation process, our own system at that stage. By the same token, if it was the other way round and we were to get someone arrested in the cells, I would research our own systems on them, but I would also be ringing the referral and assessment team or duty and say 'This person is in the cells, he has been arrested for being drunk in charge of a child – what do you know about him?' Because that assists our process when we go to CPS to say he was arrested drunk in charge of a child – 'Well, actually he is known to social services and been an open case to Joe Bloggs for six months because of issues of being drunk and leaving his child', you know. So that information is background information and which assists the CPS and whether they prosecute or not. It is a two-way process, but generally speaking I would always research our systems to see what we know about them, and on certain occasions when the referral hasn't come from social services in the first place I will be asking social services what they know. I tend not to do it so much with health, although I've got quite a good working relationship with [the hospital] which makes a huge difference ... the paediatrician and the child protection named nurse ... there is no problem with information sharing there." (Police officer 1)

Here the police officer suggests that in general all information is accepted to aid prosecution. For the police officer, received information, together with system information on the family is sought to be 'pieced' together to help with the investigative process. Information seeking behaviour from social services serves as 'background' information to help the Crown Prosecution Service (CPS) make a decision about whether to prosecute or not. Importantly, Wilson (1997) argues that those who have provided inaccurate information in the past can be regarded as unreliable sources of information, and therefore information provided by the same source in the future is likely to be disregarded The police officer suggests that information seeking from health, although not often pursued, can be helpful; in this context, she refers to the moral quality of having 'good' relationships with the hospital, and specific people within health services. She implies that 'good' relationships translate as facilitating information sharing. Meeting information need involves effort and resources that can be extensive in some instances, for example:

> "We have a duty under the law to disclose that information. Part of that disclosure process includes third-party information, which of course is social services records on file … if it is a child protection job there may be issues in the social services file which may undermine the case or even sometimes assist the case, but say for example the child has made numerous false allegations, and that is recorded in the social services file. That is information that we are duty bound to disclose to any defence, and sometimes getting that information is extremely difficult, and hard work, depending on which lawyer you speak to … which social worker you speak to … which team leader you speak to. You can have a different response every time. There is a set protocol in place for getting that information, but at times it can be very ad hoc, and it can be hard work." (Police officer 2)

The police state how they use information they receive for their role, and pass information on to the agency perceived as most relevant to 'hear' it for their respective role. This begins to raise an issue of fragmentation. Understanding perceptions of agency roles – what social workers think the police do, or what the police think social workers do – becomes important; these understandings influence what might be passed on. Salient information need is clearly information that helps professionals to do their job, but as the police officer articulates, this can be difficult. For example, the police have a particular organisational need for accuracy, especially where there is a lot of cross-referencing required. This police officer makes reference to the language of policy in building a 'picture', such that things like accuracy in spelling create an issue:

> "We set up a different record for every referral on that child, so if he gets assaulted on the Monday he will get a record there … if he gets assaulted on the Tuesday then he gets another record … so we build up a picture … although there is an issue over spelling mistakes. I do have the ability to put another name in, so if it's Smith I might put in 'Smith' you know just to try and even it out but it doesn't what we would call 'fuzzy search' if you will … there isn't that facility so we do rely very much on the accuracy of the names we are given." (Police officer 2)

The interviews with the police officers have shown that information need is role contingent, and therefore information needs (and thus types of information available for exchange) will differ from professional to professional. The police officer highlights that the police refer to children's services in order to meet their information needs, which is tied to the purpose of their role, namely policing and prosecution. We can see the information needs and behaviour of the police officer 1 in diagrammatic form in Figure 4.3.

Being part of the criminal justice system, the flowchart describes the information needs of the police officer. The police officer's needs are depicted as being solely organisational in this instance, reflecting the need for accuracy of evidence – the purpose of this is tied to the police officer's role for successful prosecution, and in passing on accurate information as evidence to the CPS.

Presented as linear for simplicity, the police officer's information-seeking behaviour may follow different pathways depending on key factors that influence whether she, as the information seeker, is satisfied or dissatisfied, thus influencing her information behaviour as an information seeker, and the actions that follow. From the police officer's account, the preferred

Figure 4.3: A police officer's information needs and behaviour

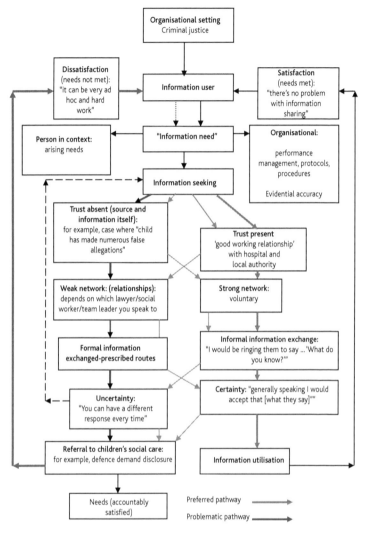

pathway is where there is trust between her and the source of information – in this case, she explains that this is present between her and social workers at children's services, and at the hospital which in turn means that such professionals within those organisations strengthen the mandated network she is part of. However, just because the network is mandated to work together and share information, the police officer suggests that this can depend on the relationships she has with professionals within those organisations (variations). When relationships are considered good, information exchange follows an informal route. In these relationships, the factor of trust is present. This enables the police officer to establish a preferred level of certainty, resulting in her information needs being satisfied because information sharing is perceived to be good with those who have the information she needs to perform her role most effectively. The police officer is dissatisfied when information exchange is "hard work".

A less desired path is where there is a lack of trust present between the police officer and other key professionals, or the source of the information (such as a child making false allegations). In these cases, levels of trust will depend on whether information from the source has proved to be reliable in the past, or on the relationship the police officer has with professionals from other organisations, which in turn can affect how certain the police officer feels, how she interprets the information received, and how she uses it. In such cases, a lack of certainty is likely to lead to a referral to children's services, a process that has the capacity to lead her to feel certain, and importantly, to fulfil her role-specific purpose of needing a disclosure within a specified timeframe to present to the CPS. However, the police officer's dissatisfaction can arise in this instance as a result of information seeking and sharing being hard work, affecting the timeliness of satisfying her information need in performing her role.

Conclusion

This chapter has sought to show the limitations of understanding information practices solely in terms of 'information sharing'. In extending a focus on systems and purpose synonymous with the information-sharing guidance by HM Government (2015b) outlined in Chapter Two, this chapter foregrounds professional needs within day-to-day information transactions between and across organisational settings. A key consideration derived from the literature in this chapter is not *how* professionals get better at sharing information, but rather what prompts them to do it at all. It is important to consider whether these prompts are indeed helpful for child protection, and how might they be improved. In child protection, professionals share information and follow 'rules' to do so, but a key question here is why do professionals want to share information in the first place? Thus, understanding 'information sharing' in terms of 'information behaviour' is helpful; professional need is a less visible dimension to these practices, which are varied and somewhat complicated. Professional needs are indeed a particular kind of information, which, as well as being role-contingent, will also differ depending on the context in which information needs emerge. The foregrounding of need shows how the referral process may be utilised to manage a number of issues, such as uncertainty and professional's affective needs, which extend beyond children and family's needs per se. Thus, identifying and understanding professional needs may help in improving information-sharing relationships across organisational settings, as well as improving referral and response services, which are inundated by referrals that may well be dealt with by alternative means.

Managers' questions for reflection

1. What different contexts can be created for professionals making referrals to children's services in which professionals affective needs can be shared (that is, passing on a hunch, feeling or anxiety; resolving uncertainty and so forth)?
2. What information grounds (other than formal case conferences, core groups and so on) can create contexts in which information sharing is most meaningfully facilitated?

Professional questions for reflection

1. Thinking about the case example given earlier in this chapter, what are your motivations for seeking or sharing information? What instances prompt you to do this?
2. Can you think of cases in which your own affective needs emerge? How do these needs affect your information behaviour? What do you do with these kinds of needs, and how might you deal with these differently?

Note
[1] See also Garfinkel (1967).

FIVE

How is information shared in 'everyday' practice?

Introduction

In Chapter Four, professional information need and information-related behaviours illustrated limitations of understanding information practices in child protection solely in terms of 'information sharing' and its focus on systems and purpose. A key consideration that emerged was not *how* professionals get better at sharing information, but rather what prompts them to do it at all. Conversely, political responses to past failings in communication and information sharing have been formulated through infrastructure reforms. Officialdom's implicit assumption has largely centred on failures in terms of both professional compliance (the actions – or inaction – of professionals) and effectiveness of protocols, procedures and information technologies. For example, the tragic death of 17-month-old Peter Connelly brought into sharp focus the deficiencies of the integrated children's system (ICS), and its contributions to the failings in the high-profile 'Baby P' case; criticisms included deadline pressures introduced by ICS, as well as excessive time needed to complete forms on the system (Wastell and White, 2014, p 144). Since the death of Peter Connelly, more sophisticated discussions (initiated by the Social Work Task Force in 2009) have taken place, urging the government to review not only the design of the ICS, but all areas of child protection practice (Wastell, 2011). Eileen Munro's review of child protection in 2011 prompted a change in direction from such received ideas, although arguably little has changed with regard to the rise in managerialism in practice (Stevenson, 2015). Professional compliance still remains at the centre of debate when things go wrong, and a child dies. Similarly, when things go wrong in healthcare, explanations for failings are framed in terms of a lack of staff compliance (Creedon, 2005) or the result of too much professional discretion and autonomy (Harrison, 1999). Thus, remedial responses that professionals need to get better at information sharing by complying more closely with more stringent procedures send out the wrong messages to managers, professionals and the public alike. From this perspective, professionals (and the public) are led to believe (with a degree of confidence) that if they behave in prescribed ways, children can be protected from harm. Thus, formal ways to perform organisational tasks are made the official indicator for measuring changes in practice, rather than trying to understand complexity of practice (Iedema et al, 2009). This indicator is not helpful. It continues to propagate public and political outrage when things go wrong and bewilderment as to how failings of communication and information sharing continue to be contributory factors in high-profile child fatalities when professionals have such detailed prescriptions to follow.

Frontline professionals are required to translate received ideas – government policies with detailed prescriptions – into action. In understanding information in terms of content and ownership, professionals are directed to consider questions such as 'What information?', 'How much information should be shared?' and 'Who should know?'. As discussed in earlier chapters, official guidance is replete with objectivist assumptions, notably an assumption of 'facts' that diligent professionals pass on to other professionals. This chapter examines received ideas surrounding professional compliance, and examines the extent to which the discourses of policy and procedure are reflected in professional talk and action. The chapter centres on questions such as 'Are professionals really non-compliant?' and 'Do professionals share in the assumptive framework and directions of official government guidance?' The chapter will explore whether and how such assumptions operate in practice, and draw conclusions about the extent to which professional assumptions converge with those made in official guidance. While the observations in this chapter may seem mundane, they are considered important for suggesting alternative 'remedial' pathways for practice development. It is important to consider by empirical means what happens within situated contexts, or is accounted for by professionals, with regard to the enactment of information-sharing policy and legislation in the everyday practice of child protection work.

The relationship between child death inquiries and information sharing

Professionals connect effective information sharing with the prevention of child death and 'near misses'. Professionals accept this relationship between effective communication, information sharing and the prevention of child death, as seen in high-profile child death cases such as that of Victoria Climbié (based on data collection pre-Peter Connelly), and described in policy guidance and legislation such as the Children Act 2004.

"I keep up to date with all the articles that are kind of going around, and obviously what went on with Victoria Climbié. I mean that was a huge issue, and I mean there was that more recent one that has put me off practising social work ... the Khyra ... the Birmingham child death case. I just don't think professionals work as closely as they should. For example, I have worked in schools and I had a small class, and two of the children were on the child protection register and I wasn't even made aware of it. I thought that was quite bad. That was in [the locality]. It was only until I started here and the family's name came up, and then I thought 'Oh I used to teach that little girl.' There is lack of communication full stop which undoubtedly has serious repercussions. It is situations where people don't share what they know, when terrible things happen and opportunities are missed, information which could have saved those children." (Assistant family support worker)

The assistant family support worker makes reference to events surrounding the Victoria Climbié case, and the severity of that case ("I mean that was a huge issue"). The worker makes further reference to the child death case of seven-year-old Khyra Ishaq in Birmingham (Birmingham LSCB, 2010). Central to the argument that the assistant family support worker makes in this instance is the issue of "lack of communication", where she states that "I just don't think professionals work as closely they should" and elaborates that "There is lack of communication full stop which undoubtedly has serious repercussions." The vocabulary used by the worker of communication and information sharing clearly echoes that of official guidance as described in detail in Chapter Two, thus showing its impact on professionals and the need for compliance in order to avoid child fatalities in the future. This is also illustrated in interviews with both a police officer in the locality's domestic violence unit (DVU) and a health professional from the local hospital's Accident and Emergency (A&E) department. First the police officer:

> "... you know, touch wood we've not had a Climbié ..., who wants one? But I do have concerns that someone will get missed. I do think it could happen in [local authority]. It could happen anywhere in the country ... you hear about tragic cases on the news, every month or so we get one. I think it is less likely now that things have moved on and information sharing is better. I mean we have had a few near misses here." (Police officer)

Assumptions again are made here regarding the relationship between child death and information sharing; again, and as with the assistant family support worker, the case of Victoria Climbié is central in formulating such an assumption. The police officer believes that a tragic case like Victoria's is less likely to happen in the locality in question as information-sharing practices are perceived as having improved. The health professional's interview describes information practices in the hospital in which she works, and those among a local network of professionals; the quality of the mandated network of professionals facilitates the timely sharing of information. Again, and similar to the police officer, the health worker makes the link between the prevention of child death through the improvement and timeliness of information sharing to avoid any children getting missed:

> "If it is anything that is particularly urgent, so say, for example, this patient we've had today, if mum had said she had a social worker, then I would ring them as a matter of courtesy and say 'This child has been brought in here and you are the social worker, you don't need to do anything urgently today but as a matter of courtesy, just to let you know they were in A&E.' With foster children and so on, the foster parents will very often ask you to do that because it is part of the contract that they let the social worker know. So you may pass things on as a matter of courtesy. If you can't get hold of them [the social worker] on that particular day, and it is vital, then you may need to get the police to follow something up. If it is not vital there and then, then the liaison health visitor will share that information with other services, other agencies first thing on the next working day. I feel that it is an excellent networking system that we have, and it creates a metaphorical net to capture all these children in on the next day, so that nothing gets missed like in Victoria Climbié, we've put this in place so that no children get missed and everything is shared." (Health professional, A&E)

Here, relationships between professionals are a key factor for facilitating information sharing. Professional compliance in sharing information is clearly not an issue for the professionals interviewed. In fact, not sharing information is perceived as 'dangerous', as the manager from a non-governmental organisation (NGO) explicitly states:

> "If anyone asks me for information about a family, and they were with us then I would give them that information – whatever they were asking for. I am

not in a position to say 'Well no I am not giving you that.' I mean I wouldn't necessarily write out every contact, and they said this, and they said that. It is only what is relevant to what they are asking for. But I wouldn't keep information because that is dangerous. That is how accidents happen."

This agency manager clearly articulates Lord Laming's imperative of complying with information-sharing obligations, as well as with *Working together* guidance (HM Government, 2015a, 2015b), and the relationship between passing on information and safeguarding children. The extract indicates that non-compliance is not an option; rather, the manager contemplates the high risks posed by not sharing information, and is therefore inclined to share whatever information is being asked so as to minimise any dangers inherent in holding on to information.

Timeliness as a key factor in 'effective' information sharing

It is possible to unpack the detail of how professionals adhere to many of the concepts and ideas of official discourse in respect of information sharing. I now draw attention to the frequently unnoticed micro-detail of practical reasoning with respect to the received vocabulary of child protection. Timely information sharing for fear of reprisals in a child death case, as emphasised in official discourse, is a very pertinent consideration, as a referral support officer highlights:

"… my bone of contention with it [dealing with referrals] is the sheer volume of work. When you have that amount of work it's hard getting the balance of doing quality work and meeting timescales. During the times that we have mammoth workloads you do worry whether you are getting it right … not getting it wrong, like missing the potential Climbiés because I haven't got all the information that the seniors need, or passed it on to them as quickly as I should of [sic]."

Agencies want to avoid being named in headlining 'tragic cases', such as that of Victoria Climbié; the referral support officer articulates this, as well as the police officer ("who wants one?") and the health professional ("so that nothing gets missed like in Victoria Climbié"). Consistent across the interview accounts is a clear impetus among diverse professionals to avoid the tragedy of 'preventable' child death and a clear adherence to official discourses of effective information sharing. There is also reference to the timing or speed of information sharing, in which 'timeliness' is a key consideration for all professionals across diverse organisational settings. In the following narrative account from an administration assistant in children's services, professional anxiety is fuelled by a concern that the information she records is not "passed on to them [senior managers] as quickly as it should be":

> "I worry every day that I have missed something or I've not put a contact on as quick as I should have or I have a fax in front of me and I don't think it is that serious yet when I've put it on it's mega, and I've messed up, and I have missed the opportunity to ask for the right information, or put it on the system as quickly as possible. The only way I can get round that is discussing every piece of post, every contact with a colleague, whether that be a family support officer, senior ... and sometimes we don't get the opportunity to do that for everything. If I don't put something on and that child is at risk, the child could be injured ... the child could be subject to further abuse or even death. You hear of children dying all the time, don't you? I don't always know one hundred per cent what has to go on straight away and what can wait so that's why you have to ask questions."

For the administrative assistant who takes initial contacts in an initial assessment team, timeliness is a key concern. The administration assistant states that not passing on contact information to senior members of staff in a timely response, either through inputting contact information on the integrated children's system (ICS) or speaking to senior colleagues directly is a problem for her, such that "the child could be injured". She maximises the impact of her concerns of timeliness by providing extreme case formulations (Pomerantz, 1986): "You hear of children dying all the time, don't you?" The professional makes a clear connection between the timeliness of passing on information and the prevention of child death. In addition, the administration assistant makes reference to having the 'right' information, or what is alternatively known as having all the 'facts'; although seemingly straightforward on the surface, getting the 'right information' (facts) is fraught with complexity. I discuss this further in the next section, using more interview extracts to illustrate the point.

Reflections of policy mantras: getting the information 'right'

Professionals are concerned with making the distinction between 'fact' and 'fiction'. This is an important process, which is underscored in professional information-sharing guidance, but is by no means an easy feat with clear demarcations. The administration assistant for children's services clearly assumes in her account that there is 'right' information out there to be found, from which we can also deduce, by implication, that she accepts that there is 'wrong' information (Sack, 1992). Establishing the 'right' information permits the action of sharing information, a consideration articulated by an education welfare officer:

> "… we do particularly with schools get a lot of hearsay information which can be difficult. So it can be, what we wouldn't do is ignore it. What we would be doing is visiting the home and trying ways to address it, or find out what we could. But particularly from schools we do get a lot of information particularly from teachers which will be personal judgements and you will say 'Well how do you know that?' and it's 'Well, er we don't, but we think it.' We are looking to evidence base it but we

would retain the knowledge, try to find out about it to make sure it's right, factual information, and then share it as a matter of course."

The education welfare officer makes reference to "hearsay information which can be difficult". However, knowing this information cannot be ignored, but rather for this type of information to be 'right' or not, requires a process of verification ("visiting the home and trying ways to address it, or find out what we could") in which, collectively as an agency, they "are looking to evidence base it, but we would retain the knowledge, try to find out about it to make sure it's right, factual information". The translation between 'hearsay' and 'factual information' is an important process; it is only 'facts' that can be shared "as a matter of course". Thus, establishing 'facts' is an important element in information sharing. Factual information was also shown to be a very important feature for an NGO manager facilitating information sharing with children's services:

> **R (researcher)**: "Right, OK, so what information do you need to confidently refer to social services?"

> **M (NGO manager)**: "Facts! Yes. It is how it is clearly recorded. Yeah it's facts. Sometimes you can give them [social services] the facts and they are not interested."

> **R**: "What are facts, and how do you get those facts?"

> **M**: "What we see and hear. We get the facts from working with children and families, and checking out with other agencies. It is meetings, telephone calls, seeing chronologies. Chronologies are fantastic things. I love chronologies, I do, I do, honestly. If you've got a chronology on a file, you know what should have happened to those children. We have seen them ... 40 pages long and we still didn't do anything."

The NGO manager states that clearly presented 'facts' are what she needs in order to confidently share information with social services (although social services do not always appear to be interested in the 'facts' that she has passed on to them). When asked to elaborate on her meaning of the word 'facts' and how 'facts' are established, the manager states that they are "What we see and hear…. It is meetings, telephone calls, seeing chronologies", and are established by the work her agency carries out with "children and families", and validating what is seen or heard by "checking out with other agencies". The manager places great importance on the usefulness of chronologies in seeing the 'facts' and interpreting those 'facts' by retrospectively being able to see in a documented format "what should have happened to those children … and we still didn't do anything". Importantly, 'facts' as unproblematically characterised here, denote a static quality – an 'endpoint' – suggesting that information has a stable or fixed meaning similar to policy, which is certainly not the case, as the next chapter will show. The manager's sentiments follow those echoed in serious case reviews and public inquiries of 'error and blame' (Broadhurst et al, 2009) and issues of professional compliance, emphasising what professionals failed to do, and, *retrospectively*, what they should have done.

Procedural relationships: 'who' to pass on information to and 'when'

Contrary to received ideas echoed in serious case reviews and public inquiries, professionals do understand the procedures for passing on information, and comply with the demands set by their agency, and more broadly, with child welfare information-sharing protocol. A number of professional narratives highlight that compliance with information-sharing requirements is necessary and is adhered to. For the police service, responding and sharing information in prescribed ways is a mandatory requirement that is closely linked to performance management demands, as a police officer explains here:

"[I]nformation is mandatory. It is monitored. It is a performance indicator … completeness, trails of logs, risk assessment. Basically we close a log of when all the component parts are brought together … it's been assessed correctly, it has been given a risk score, the enquiries that needed to be done have been done, the information in relation to children, victims, and offender have been put on, and then it can be closed. As I say that is judged as a performance indicator at local and county level. It is about compliance really. We are always sort of looking for people we should be sharing information with, but the baseline is that the statutory bodies such as health and social services are always told that a child has been identified at the scene. It is an automatic response, we have to do it, and we do it. What we have is an information-sharing facility on our database, and so you basically complete your nominal. You complete your incident and tie it to the previous incidents. You then hit an information-sharing button and it generates a form. It is then cut and pasted onto an email and sent, just like that, one, two, and its gone." (Police officer, DVU)

The police officer quoted here states that information sharing is work, and further, a compulsory element of his work as a police officer in the DVU. The police officer has no option but to comply, as recorded information is used to monitor the performance of his agency (the police service). The police officer describes the active role his agency takes in seeking out people that *should* have the information his agency holds, although he states that sharing information with social services and health is a mandatory activity. Further reference is made to the timeliness that information is shared with these agencies ("one, two, and it's gone"), as suggested in earlier interview accounts. This process is facilitated by an electronic information-sharing facility on his department's computer database. For the police officer, compliance with information-sharing procedures are traceable and visible for others to see. Following procedures for sharing information is again highlighted by an NGO worker:

"… two girls, self-referral … came in as being sexually abused. That was apparently the whole issue but it wasn't, it was domestic abuse. The family were falling apart in front of our eyes. We made a referral to children's services because the child clearly stated she had a bruise. She came in and clearly disclosed what had happened. I spoke to dad, and dad initially denied it, and then kind of said he did it, sort of, 'Alright I hold my hands up.' We didn't want the blue lights flashing. He knew he did wrong, and he was willing to work with us. He was working with us. We made a referral to social services the next day. This was happening at 5pm. I had assessed the situation and the children were safe. They were going home with dad, dad was alright, and the kids were OK going home. The next day we made a referral to social services and didn't even get a phone call back. They went out and did a Section 47, but too heavy-handed, I thought.

The NGO worker provides a specific case example where she has complied with procedures by fulfilling her obligations for sharing information with social services in a timely response, after a child has suffered an injury. She knows the action social services will take 'a Section 47' (as this child has suffered an injury the local authority has a duty to carry out a child protection investigation),[1] and interestingly still complies with the following procedures even though she does not entirely agree with social services' response in dealing with this case: "We didn't want the blue lights flashing…. They went out and did a Section 47, but too heavy-handed, I thought." The worker was asked why this particular case was referred to social services when the children had been assessed by the worker as being safe, and dad was seen to comply with the agency's request to work with them, to which the NGO worker replied "there was an injury and that is part of our protocol to pass it on". Despite seen as not a necessary or appropriate response, the worker adheres to protocol as it expected of her. Sharing similar sentiments to that of the NGO worker, a deputy head teacher from a secondary school expresses the need to procedurally pass on information as a matter of course:

> "[W]e have to get down to the fact that if there are concerns then we have to refer it on … that's what we are told to do … it's like a hot potato … we can't deal with it legally, properly and all the rest of it and that's why we have to pass it on. But all social services say is 'Have you rung the parents?' and often I say 'No I haven't.' I mean the legalities of the system are that you refer significant concerns, and if you don't then you are in deep water, aren't you?"

The deputy head teacher makes reference to the legal responsibilities her agency has in passing on concerns. She situates the repercussions of not doing something within the legal parameters of safeguarding children. She uses the metaphor of a 'hot potato', emphasising the timeliness required to pass on concerns to avoid the school, as an agency getting their 'hands burnt', so to speak. In other words, the deputy head teacher understands the potential and serious ramifications if information is not shared.

Central to her argument, the deputy head invokes a legal reason why information of this nature has to be shared with social services: "we can't deal with it legally … properly and all the rest of it and that's why we have to pass it on". The teacher highlights social services' response in receiving her referrals, whereby they make sure that she has followed procedures by notifying the parents of the referral, although the teacher does not acknowledge this as a legal imperative in the same way as social services (she often says 'no'): "But all social services say is 'Have you rung the parents?' and often I say 'No, I haven't'" Later on, the deputy head states that she is required to follow this procedure before social services will accept the referral. She further provides her reasons for her not doing so: "We have to see parents everyday which is why we don't want to do it … it affects our relationship with parents, but we still have to follow the rules so social services will accept it." Although the teacher does not fully comply with procedures per se, she is encouraged by social services to 'follow the rules' when passing on information by the formalised route of sharing information via making a referral. With regard to sharing the advice from social services in following procedures and notifying parents before sharing information, a health visitor comments:

"Health visitors keep 'cause for concern' in their records and because I am not GP-based it is important that I share that information with anyone else who is involved with that family, so I send a copy of that cause for concern to the GP and I would send it to any other health professional that is involved, so if I'm dealing with a family that is registered with a GP or they are not … as soon as they are registered I will forward a copy of my cause for concern to the GP. I will send it to the health visitor that is attached to that GP surgery. I will send it to the school nurse. I will send it to education, Sure Start[2], health visitor, midwife, women's unit, so that my picture of concerns are clear for everybody to see. I will have obviously told the family that I'm doing that 'cos that's what we have to do, but that will be very clearly documented so that I know that I've shared that information correctly as guidance clearly outlines, and that I'm doing everything I can for that family."

The health visitor states the importance of sharing 'cause for concern' information with other agencies, and provides a list of professionals that she would share those concerns with. The inclusion of 'obviously' within her statement is important; she states that notifying families is something she has to do before sharing information with other professionals, and therefore it is common sense that she follows what she is formally instructed to do. The health visitor echoes Lord Laming's imperative of passing on clear information "so that my picture of concerns are clear for everybody to see". Furthermore, explicit reference is made to sharing "information correctly as guidance clearly outlines".

Making reference to domestic abuse policy and sharing information with other agencies as part of procedure, a civilian working in the DVU comments:

> "OK, well, DV policy is like ... we won't leave a couple that argue. If we go round and they say 'Yes we were arguing but we are not doing it now' we would say 'That is not our problem, one of you is leaving the address', and we would remove one of them. If they can't go and stay at friends and relatives, even if it is just for the night there is a possibility that we would have to arrest them for breach of the peace. The referral to other agencies is part of the procedure for us processing it. That is usually the final stage with it. So from that point it is closed for us."

This final illustration from the civilian provides an example of how domestic violence information-sharing policy is enacted in practice. The civilian states that making a referral, as a formalised procedure for sharing information, "is part of the procedure for us processing it". Following this procedure is important for the police, as it is at the point of sharing information that the information is no longer 'owned' by the DVU; the responsibility of the information has shifted to the agencies that the information has been shared with. In other words, an 'endpoint' is reached for the DVU as the referring agent. 'Endpoints' to information are an important feature in child protection information practices, an area that will be pursued in greater depth in the next chapter.

Conclusion

The interview extracts presented in this chapter have shown that professionals, in terms of how they account for their practices, share an assumptive framework of official discourses, and adhere to many of the concepts and ideas contained within them. For some professionals interviewed, the death of Victoria Climbié and the recommendations regarding effective information sharing were acutely relevant to their practice. In most current practices, however, the deaths of Peter Connelly, Daniel

Pelka, Hamza Khan and Keanu Williams now permeate child protection practices rather than that of Victoria Climbié. Recent research by White and colleagues (2015) has found that the publicity surrounding cases of child death such as that of Daniel Pelka has directly affected professional consciousness, and has had an impact on organisational culture (p 29). As a consequence, professionals subscribe to the received truths and the vocabulary of official documents, in which the association between the prevention of child deaths and effective information-sharing is central.

Professionals clearly articulate that they want to avoid being involved in child fatalities, leading them to work in prescribed ways as detailed by government policies, procedures and guidance. Who can blame them? However, professional narrative accounts that describe compliance are important because they are at variance with messages from public inquiries that suggest the reverse. A recurrent theme in public inquiries is that professionals are often non-compliant or do not carry out their roles as effectively as directed in information-sharing protocols. This is also the case in healthcare. By contrast, the interview extracts in this chapter not only describe compliance with procedures, but also reveal that the received vocabulary of official guidance is embedded in professional talk, in the context of timeliness, establishing 'fact' from 'opinion', and a concern with getting the 'right' information. Given this level of professional compliance, why do information-sharing practices appear to fail, and repeated errors occur? If, as interviews suggest, professionals follow stringent rules, procedures and obligations, where and how does information sharing across multi-agency settings fall short?

In the next chapter, I begin to answer this question by charting some micro-observations of the 'indeterminate zones of practice' (Klein, 2004, p 4). This will draw attention to the complexities of information sharing that have hitherto been absent from detailed interrogation to date. The next chapter shows that professionals have a range of methods that draw on formal procedures as well as informal heuristics that are less visible aspects of information-sharing activity in child protection practices.

Managers' questions for reflection

1. How can 'good' information-sharing practices be strengthened across agencies?
2. What practical measures do you think could be taken to mitigate any problems that are identified by frontline professionals in current information-sharing practices?

Professional questions for reflection

1. Can you describe the characteristics of 'good' and 'bad' information-sharing practices?
2. Are there any obstacles that inhibit getting the information you need? If so, what are these obstacles, and what causes them? How do you overcome these obstacles?
3. Do you consider there to be 'right' or 'wrong' information? If so, can you describe how you know that information is either 'right' or 'wrong'?
4. Has following procedures resulted in actions that you consider inappropriate? What outcome were you seeking? Was this clearly articulated? If not, why?

Notes

[1] Under Section 47 of the Children Act (1989), where there is reasonable cause to suspect that a child is suffering or likely to suffer significant harm, the local authority is required to carry out enquiries to decide whether action should be taken to safeguard and promote the welfare of the child.

[2] Sure Start centres are children's centres across the UK set up to improve outcomes for disadvantaged children and families with greatest need.

SIX

Putting pieces of the 'jigsaw' together to establish a 'full' picture

Introduction

The previous chapter explored compliance with information-sharing rules and requirements through interviews with professionals. Attention was drawn to professionals' concerns in establishing a 'full' picture of a child's life by connecting the 'right pieces' of information, as if completing a jigsaw puzzle. This chapter examines 'jigsaw' *practices* observed and documented in day-to-day child protection work. Empirical data used in this chapter highlights that there is something of a mismatch between the conceptual, jigsaw metaphor and jigsaw *practices* that operate on the ground. Conceptually, the 'jigsaw' engenders notions of 'connectedness' or 'interlocking' pieces, and in this respect, the metaphor is found to cohere with practices. However, where the abstract metaphor falls short is in the notion of a 'finite' or 'full' picture that is achievable *sui generis*. Inevitably, and as shown in Chapter Three, the 'full' picture' will always be situated in and subject to ongoing revision, meaning that the 'full' picture' confounds objectivist policy dictates in its suggestion that it has a stable meaning. Indeed, what I will show in this chapter is quite the contrary: when practices are scrutinised through post hoc interview accounts from various professionals, the very stability of jigsaw *pieces* themselves is drawn into question.

The political resonance of securing a 'full' picture

The notion of securing a 'full' picture is pervasive within child protection discourse, and is clearly manifest in official policy guidance. Securing a 'full' picture is said to be achieved only through multi-agency working, as outlined in the progress report following the death of 17-month-old Peter Connelly in the London Borough of Haringey:

> It is clear that most staff in social work, youth work, education, police, health, and other frontline services are committed to the principle of inter-agency working, and recognise that children can only be protected effectively when all agencies pool information, expertise, and resources so that a full picture of the child's life is better understood. (Laming, 2009, p 36)

The prevailing message in high-profile inquiry reports into child deaths, including that of Peter Connelly, is that if a 'full' picture of the children's lives had been ascertained by professionals such tragedies may have been prevented. In supporting this claim further, Reder and Duncan (2003) have retrospectively commented that, according to the majority of public inquiries, professionals in the cases examined have failed to gain a 'full' picture of a child's life, either because certain information was lacking, or because professionals did not actively seek information beyond their own involvement in a case. In the most recent HM Government *Working together* document in March 2015, the notion of establishing a 'full' picture emerges again in Section 16, thus showing no sign of fading away from multi-agency guidance:

> No single professional can have a full picture of a child's needs and circumstances and, if children and families are to receive the right help at the right time, everyone who comes into contact with them has a role to play in identifying concerns,

> sharing information and taking prompt action. (HM Government, 2015a)

In pursuit of a 'full' picture, information from a variety of multi-agency professionals is somewhat *naively* expected to be pieced together so that the 'right' children and families receive a service in a timely fashion. In the language of the 'jigsaw' in child protection, and the guidance cited above, professionals in individual agencies do not have *all* the 'pieces' to establish a 'full' picture. Rather, the jigsaw is assembled by relevant professionals working together to bring to the table their own 'piece' or 'pieces' (Payne, 2008) to create a 'full' picture of vulnerable children's lives.

The jigsaw metaphor

A jigsaw metaphor is now well established in child protection work and provides professionals with a generalised framework of meaning for carrying out information-related activities such as sharing 'relevant' information in contributing to a case. The jigsaw metaphor emerged in the context of the 'Cleveland scandal' of 1987, which put child sexual abuse firmly on the child protection agenda (DH, 1988), and emphasised the 'putting together' of key pieces of information in complex sexual abuse cases (Frothingham et al, 1993). In detecting and dealing with sexual abuse, the 'jigsaw' denoted the bringing together of skills, knowledge and perspectives of other professionals in the pursuit of a 'full' picture (Hobbs et al, 1995a). This jigsaw metaphor subsequently found articulation with respect to sudden infant death syndrome (SIDS) and other forms of child maltreatment such as neglect (Hobbs et al, 1995b).

In child protection work, social workers are viewed as being central in this jigsaw activity, their role being to put together 'pieces' of information, to make decisions based on the picture assembled, and to act in accordance with what the picture represents. Unlike the more simple and traditional jigsaw puzzle, professionals do not have the advantage of working from an illustrated picture on the front of a box. They cannot be certain about what each piece looks like, whether they have the pieces that fit the jigsaw, and consequently what picture of a child or family will emerge once pieces have been put together (Munro, 1996). However, professionals do have an idea of what kind of picture they are looking for – their background picture deriving from previous case work and underpinned by a dominant ideology of child 'abuse' (Parton, 1997). Professionals operate on the basis of 'background expectancies' (Taylor and White, 2000) and 'templates'; while these are not fixed, they derive from a blending of textbook knowledge, media images and situated practices. By 'blending' these elements, professionals are able to create a 'full' picture of children and families lives. In beginning to understand what a health visitor's jigsaw may look like in determining child neglect, Lewin and Herron (2007, p 97) provide an illustration of what constitutes pieces of this professions jigsaw, as shown in Table 6.1.

Table 6.1: The 'jigsaw' in the diagnosis of neglect

Problem denial by parents (who may have learning difficulties).	History from child – bullied, friendless, aggressive.	'Attention seeking'; concern by nursery and school about standards of care.
Physical symptons eg, pain from dental caries; Developmental delay eg, language and social skills.	Poor physical condition – dirty, thin hair, nappy rash; Poor compliance with medical treatment eg, asthma.	Growth – stunted/fails to reach potential height; Increased risk of accidents: RTA, fire, drowning.
Little effect from supportive networks since family and friends may share similar problems.	Poverry with poor housing, diet, parents with poor physical and mental health, limited education.	Large numbers of professionals involved – health visitor, school nurse, social worker, GP, paediatrician, housing department.

Source: Adapted from Hobbs and Wynne (2002)

The table provides guidance for health visitors about 'relevant' pieces of information for determining child neglect. It tells health visitors which pieces of the 'jigsaw' they need to assemble in order to get the 'full' picture (history, physical condition and so forth). Adapted from early work by Hobbs et al (1995a, 1995b), the descriptive text that accompanies this table offers advice to professionals concerning the diagnosis of neglect, and indicates that this diagnosis is achievable through the sum of the jigsaw pieces and the 'final' picture it creates. A 'final' picture denotes that an endpoint to information gathering and analysis can be reached, premised on objectivist assumptions about the social world. As this book suggests throughout, such a notion is both naive and problematic, but this has not prevented it from becoming an enduring metaphor in the child protection discourse, 'seeping' into the training manuals of a multi-agency professional workforce. Having discussed the jigsaw in theoretical terms, it is now time to explore its relevance, as well as how the dominant metaphor *actually* works from the perspectives of a variety of professionals in frontline practice.

Using empirical data to think differently about 'pieces' of professional jigsaws

In examining the narrative accounts of a diverse number of professionals tasked with safeguarding and promoting the welfare of children, it is evident that the jigsaw metaphor is very much present in the everyday of professional information practices. Professionals describe the process of piecing information together, akin to assembling a jigsaw, in trying to ascertain a 'full' picture of children's lives. Looking more closely at how this operates in practice, professionals describe a process that requires much revision and translation, a complex activity involving a process of sense making and connection, as the following extract shows:

"A lot of referrals we would make to social services are if a child has been harmed or they have been hurt, like a physical injury. We had a child who started our school. She had come from Newcastle way and had a scar right down her face. Her parents … the trouble is they put down a father … they put this name down and it's never the father, and they have lost their birth certificates and stuff like that. Anyway, she came to our school and the parents were immaculate. You know mum was immaculate, dad was immaculate. They were asking all the right questions, and you know she came in and she always looked quite neat and everything. Mum was very neat and tidy, and there was a younger brother. Anyway, when she came into school we asked her what had happened to her face and it turned out … this is a long time before that she had been out riding on her bike down a hill and when she went to put her brakes on they didn't work and she went straight into a lamppost and cut her face … you know, it was a massive scar. We thought that was that, but it didn't sound good. It didn't fit in with how the parents looked at all. Anyway, as she came in it started that no one would pick her up and then, well they did pick her up but there were often times where she was late, or there were times when she would come into school very, very upset but she wouldn't say very much. Then it came out that there were lots of people in her house at night and then other children used to come in and say that lots of things were going on. It got to the stage where she was talking about changing the baby's nappy. Then she would say she couldn't get up in the morning. Then eventually I think she came in and said that her little brother had to go to hospital, spiked himself with a needle. Some point there the picture had gathered that something was going on there and it was referred to social services, and in actual fact she was drug dealing and that became one of the houses they (police) raided and closed, but you would never have known by the initial. You had to wait to build up a full picture." (Primary school head teacher)

The head teacher is describing here a case of a newly enrolled child at her school who had moved to the town from a different part of England. First, the teacher is describing the kinds of information that her school passes on to children's services: "if a child has been harmed or they have been hurt, like a physical injury". Physical injury is a 'picture' recognised by health and social care professionals and is derived from a background picture of child 'abuse'. It is a gloss, similar to a portrait or a landscape, where most people agree upon its significance but it is nonetheless open to interpretation. As a type of 'picture', it may be contested, but there is agreement within the literature on physical injury that it is a picture; its signs (pieces) are perceived as being clear and more easily documentable (a bruise or broken bones, for example) and qualitatively different from other kinds of abuse such as sexual abuse (Frothingham et al, 1993). However, in this case, physical injury is ambiguous; as the head teacher's story unfolds, it becomes clear that there is a question mark over whether a 'massive scar' present on the child's face signifies child 'abuse'. By making reference to the 'massive scar' down the child's face, the child is immediately categorised as being 'visibly' different from other children, and, given the nature of the injury, a potential candidate for child protection services. Despite the persuasive notion that the signs of physical injury are somewhat straightforward in the work of diagnosing and identifying child 'abuse', the head teacher's account highlights that it is the 'meaning' that is attributed to the physical injury that is the deciding factor for action (that is, making a referral to children's services). Although the scar has a material reality, it is the *sense* that the teacher makes of the scar that 'counts' in this context. The initial 'surface' reading of the scar (based on the scar's material properties) is seen as an indicative sign of child 'abuse' or neglect. However, the parents provide a 'reasonable' account for the cause of the scar (a bike accident), and this account, together with other observations by the head teacher ("the parents were immaculate…. They were asking all the right questions, and you know she came in and she always looked quite neat and everything"), leads to a revision of the initial reading of the scar. The scar as a 'piece' of a potential child 'abuse' picture or jigsaw has a material reality, but the meaning attributed to the scar is unstable, and as the account unfolds, the meaning is seen to shift. Connecting information or 'pieces' produces this or that reading of the scar, and the meaning depends on the sense that is made of it within different contexts; information arising further down the line has the potential to re-cast earlier interpretations that the head teacher has made. Here, the scar on the child's face, as an initial signifier of child 'abuse', does not fit with the head teacher's observations of the parents (they are "immaculate"), given the teacher's background expectancies regarding maltreating parents. Later the head teacher describes how the child's own account is given further credence through the appearance of the parents and also by the fact that they asked "all the right questions". The disjuncture between the initial appearance of the child, and the subsequent presentation of the parents and their accounts, is momentarily put to one side ("that was that"), despite the reservations on the part of the teacher ("but it didn't sound good"). It is only when further incoming information is received that the head teacher's picture undergoes a further shift ("I think she came in and said that her little brother had to go into hospital, spiked himself with a needle"); here, her initial suspicions are rekindled. The needle incident with the child's sibling is the catalyst piece that both validates her suspicions noted earlier and is also deemed the 'right' piece that warrants passing on her 'jigsaw' to children's services in the form of a referral. The referral she makes to children's services reflects a child 'abuse'/neglect picture that has been produced from the connections of 'pieces' she has made (such as the scar on the child's face, lost birth certificates, parents late picking the child up from school and the child getting upset). More importantly, her concerns are constructed retrospectively as a result of constant revision, and ongoing analysis of the case. Thus, what emerges is a process that is *non-linear*; the meaning of 'pieces' is always indexical – information arising further on down the line has the potential to recast earlier interpretations. There are indeed a number of 'pictures' at any given point in time, or more aptly a picture in motion – a drama unfolds that rewrites earlier 'pieces' in terms of their meaning or definition. However, not all professionals are able to build a picture on their own, as a deputy head teacher of a secondary school explains:

> "Through the child's performance in school, through the child's behaviour, through what the child says, what the friends of the child say … through parents and through teachers, through extended school, people outside of school. So people coming in saying there is this situation and it is only going to be that little tiny piece of the jigsaw and it is sort of up to someone else to put all those pieces together and say 'Is there a problem here, yes there is, no there isn't.'

> If it's just that then that's fine, OK, I will leave that, that is not a problem and I can deal with it, but that could be the key to a whole can of worms so we have to investigate that key, and we may only know that little bit of information, but I find that if I refer that little bit of information on, that suspicion … then if nothing else comes from it then that's OK, but it could be that behind that there is a whole load of things that we didn't know about."

Drawing attention to the importance of 'connections' between many 'pieces' that enable a picture to be produced, the teacher acknowledges the limits in her capacity to build a picture of her own, given that only 'snippets' of information are available to her. Sometimes, agents of the school are just passing on a "suspicion" or a "little bit of information", behind which a "whole can of worms" may be revealed once the suspicion has been passed on, implying that something may 'lay beneath' the surface (Howe, 1996) of a suspicion. Based on this premise and the teacher's reasoning, 'pieces' have to be referred on to another agency to secure a 'full' picture.

Organisational relevance and context, and building a 'full' picture

So far, from the two teachers' narratives, we have learnt that as a profession, teachers are limited with regard to the kinds of information they can ever be privy to, because the private world of the child and his/her family lies beyond the scope of their professional role. Teachers can build up a picture within the context of the school, in terms of presenting aspects of a child's behaviour and noting what the friends of the child say, but beyond that, the case must be passed on for further investigation. Illustrated very clearly here is that building up a 'full' picture does not comprise gathering pieces that are universally available to a multi-professional workforce, but rather that building a 'full' picture is situated. In other words, each professional assembles the bits that are 'available' within his or her particular context and have relevance as indicators of child concern within that particular organisation or context, as one social worker explains:

> "Some information might be more relevant to us because it is a snippet and it's intelligence so we might be able to link it to something else which then becomes the bigger picture, you know. Because by the very nature of what happens, it tends to be secretive anyway, yeah. So if someone comes in with some partial information albeit someone in a children's home saying 'Johnny is coming back to the children's home, new mobile phone, new trainers all the time, he is picked up from the end of the drive', now who would be bothered about that information before? The police would have said 'So what?' before. We would say 'OK, what do we know about who he is associating with?' We may or may not decide to raise awareness within the home, the staff there about young people ... so perhaps you may need to think holistically about what might be going on, is he out shop lifting or is he basically being involved with an older male who is giving him new trainers, mobile phone, and he is involved in rent boy stuff, and that's the kind of thing to be honest that happens to very mundane pieces of information." (Social worker, non-governmental organisation)

This social worker is part of a multidisciplinary team whose organisational focus is the sexual exploitation of children and young people. In this interview account, the social worker describes how a 'full' picture is assembled and, more importantly, describes how identifying pieces is context-specific or situated (within the criminal justice system, in this case). The social worker defines 'pieces' of his agency's 'full' picture in terms of the noun 'intelligence', which reflects the agency in which he is situated and its organisational objectives (the nature of sexual exploitation and his observation of how it tends to be 'secretive'). Attention is drawn to 'pieces' that he, as part of an agency, sees as relevant but what other professionals might not have seen as relevant in the past ("who would be bothered about that information before?"). The agency in which he is situated positions him to attribute meaning to 'mundane' information that other professionals would not understand in the same way. He tells us something about the social worker's 'picture' that the police did not have before the agency was set up ("The police would have said 'So what?' before"). His use of the word 'mundane' is important here: it implies that 'pieces' viewed as 'ordinary' or 'unimportant' in another setting are key to understanding the picture in this particular context. Thus, the process of attributing meaning to incoming information is bound by organisational relevance; a 'piece' can be depicted in a myriad of ways, although it is organisational relevance that determines 'what' meaning is attributed to a 'piece' and the connections that are made between pieces in assembling a 'full' picture.

Receiving a referral: translation, meaning and the instability of 'pieces'

'Pieces' that are deemed relevant get passed on and are acted on in different ways according to organisational relevance. There is, however, a further complexity to jigsaw practices at the referral stage. This relates to the process of *translation*, which operates on a number of levels. As discussed in Chapter Three, making a referral is the formal procedure or the official term for sharing information. The process is essentially a dialogue between collaborating agencies and children's social care through which the referring agency passes on to the 'receiver' a 'version' of the presenting needs of children and their families. In communication with the referrer, the receiver then acts on this information to produce, in the first instance, an agency-relevant recording of the referral. It involves the transaction of 'information' in such a way that befits the receiving organisation. As a social and interactive process, a number of professionals positioned within their agencies act on and 'test out' their concerns 'in transit' about a child (similar to a hypothesis), which requires an ongoing, process of translation back and forth. However, translation work continues as further work is required on the part of the professional or agency receiving the referral.

Social workers carry the authority to finally determine the 'final' picture through the translation process, as a senior practitioner from children's services illustrates:

> "Right, so it's a young child. It's come from health visitor, they have suggested it's a possible S47, but obviously that's just their thought and not what I see as yet. Right, she is saying it's emotional abuse caused by domestic violence, both physical and emotional risk of physical injury, for me there is not enough information there [on the ICS system] to make a call. I don't know what that means, a risk of physical injury. I mean, I want to know why they are giving me that statement ... what evidence they've got to back up that statement. I want to know who they've spoken to and hopefully this will give me the information I need to think that, yes, this is a CP concern and warrants our intervention. I need to open this up as a referral as the health visitor is not giving me everything I need to know, just bits. I need to get a full picture of what's going on to know if there are real concerns here that meets our threshold, or the case can be closed."

Here, the senior practitioner is talking though a possible 'Section 47' child protection enquiry under the Children Act (1989) child protection investigation from a health visitor that has arrived in her 'inbox'. A decision on this contact has to be made by the end of the working day (either opened up as a referral, or closed with no further action). The practitioner's response to the health visitor's written contact is to search for further substantiation on the claims being made by the health visitor. She clearly indicates that at this point this is the health visitor's account only and not yet her version of events ("that's just their thought and not what I see as yet"), implying that until she secures the meaning of the health visitor's 'pieces' underpinning the referral, the picture presented remains uncertain. The senior practitioner highlights her part in the process – the seniority of her role and the credibility conferred by her employer organisation gives her the ultimate authority to secure the meaning of 'pieces' and assemble the 'final' picture performing her senior role under the guise of her organisation provides unwritten organisational entitlement, or authority in securing the meaning of 'pieces' and the 'final' picture that is assembled. This is a very fundamental point. Both the deputy head teacher's and the senior practitioner's narrative suggest that there is a 'hierarchy' or unofficial entitlement in terms of who secures the 'final' meaning the 'pieces' to create the 'final' version of a picture – this is considered to be the privilege of social workers, both by other professionals and by social workers themselves.

Reaching an 'endpoint' and passing on an assumed 'full' picture

The head teacher's actions described earlier in the chapter are organised around an assumed 'endpoint', at which there is either a sufficient picture that warrants the action of passing on information in the form of a referral, or putting it to one side as unsubstantiated. The example of the child with the scar highlights that this head teacher's 'endpoint' was reached with the discovery of the 'right piece' of the jigsaw ("Then eventually I think she came in and said that her little brother had to go to hospital, spiked himself with a needle"). This enabled her to pass on her picture to children's services for investigation ("the picture had gathered that something was going on there and it was referred"). However, despite the head teacher reaching her assumed 'endpoint', it is important to note here that the child's situation, aside from a referral having been made, remains essentially the same. The only thing that has changed is that the head teacher now has a 'picture of concern' about this child's life that she then passes on. However, in her use of the language of policy, assembling a 'full' picture takes time to achieve ("you would have never known by the initial. You had to wait to build up a full picture"). The idea that a 'full' picture is out there to be gained is further suggested by a social worker in the following extract:

"We've had children's homes ringing in saying 'We've got concerns about such a body', and that would lead to us piecing information together. I think it's only when you put all the information together to make the complete jigsaw, can you then see what's really happening. The cases we've had have started with very little pieces of information, you know, and in that sense it has meant that people have been locked up who are involved in abusing more than one young person. That's why when we are doing the visits, you see holistically who else is involved so you don't just concentrate on the person that the complaint's about. Who does that young person associate with? Who is her peer group? Have they been involved with this person? And you go around and the first five might say 'No nothing has happened to me, I'm OK.' Number 6 might say 'Actually he has done it to me as well' so that means that the case is going to have a better chance of getting a prosecution because you've got corroboration, but it also means that you check who might be at risk, or who has been at risk of this person, you know. In a way you are opening up the can of worms and discovering things, rather than what has already happened sometimes, you know." (Social worker, non-governmental organisation)

This social worker is describing the process of assembling an organisationally relevant jigsaw, his reasons for doing so, and when an 'endpoint' is reached. Because of where the social worker is positioned, and the relevance of information for his organisation, an 'endpoint' is reached when a 'full' picture is thought to be had; this is at the point of corroboration and prosecution. The social worker provides an example of an assumed reality or a 'correct' version of what is *really* happening ("I think it's only when you put all the information together to make the complete jigsaw, can you then see what's really happening"). Similar to Pollner's (1987) assertion, there is an assumption by the social worker that if others follow the same pattern of investigation, they too will find out what is 'really' going on or have access to the same underlying reality. The less visible aspects of sense making, translation in context and organisational relevance tell us otherwise, and therefore defies such logic or possibility. However, because of where he is situated, the social worker is in a position to carry out an investigative role (similar to the police) and establish what has 'happened', or is able to check out what his agency thinks is happening. This is very different for other professionals situated in other agencies, such as teachers, whose role and position does not allow them to perform investigatory actions in the same way.

Conclusion

This chapter has shown that there is something of a mismatch between the jigsaw as articulated in conceptual abstract accounts and jigsaw practices on the ground. As an abstract metaphor, the jigsaw does not reflect the complexities of building a 'full' picture in practice. The 'jigsaw' engenders notions of 'connectedness' of pieces, and in this respect, the metaphor appears to cohere with child welfare practices. However, where it falls short is in capturing the complexity of processes such as sense making, connection and translation in context in frontline practices. Decisions about what information is a signifier of concern, what information should be shared and when, require difficult and complex judgements to be made by professionals working with children and families. The inherently uncertain and unpredictable nature of family life means that making sense of information is complex. Fixed representations of children's lives are only achieved at particular points in time, for example, through words on a page (words on a referral form, in an electronic record, in a case file and so forth), but their reality is fleeting and, therefore, subject to further interpretation and review. As such, pictures are in flux and are therefore more like 'motion' pictures than the 'full' pictures referred to by Laming (2003) and the most recent *Working together* information-sharing guidance (HM Government, 2015b). For example, as shown at the beginning of the chapter in the head teacher's interview extract, the scar that the head teacher makes reference to, and which holds great significance in her account, does not have *in situ* a 'fixed' property vis-à-vis a diagnosis of child 'abuse'. In other words, the scar on a child's face is an accident in one context, but a non-accidental injury in another context, in terms of the meaning attributed to it. We learn from the teacher that meaning making is always in process and has a temporal quality, in that meaning is both achieved at particular points in time and can also change in time and place. Arguably, the only constant that can be taken from the teacher's account (aside from a referral having been made) is the child's circumstances, which essentially remains the same. The only thing that is seen to change is the head teacher's 'picture of concern' over time.

In critically reflecting on the data presented in this chapter, we need to focus on sense making – the connections that are drawn between what is observed and and what is influenced by context. Moreover, professionals need to reflect on their actions of 'connecting', that is, the connections they make and how these connections build 'full' pictures. However, connecting pieces, and assembling a 'full' picture is potentially problematic if considering Luhmann's theoretical account of 'autopoietic discourse' – an attempt at 'blending pieces' together to create a 'full' picture does not necessarily illuminate new or richer ways of knowing a child's circumstances, but rather can create confusion in translating the 'pieces' into something that the receiving agent can 'hear', something that is not 'noise' (Luhmann, cited in King and Piper, 1995). A practical implication of this is that things *can* get 'lost in translation', something that was clear from the evidence submitted by health and social services during the inquiry following the death of Victoria Climbié (White, 2009) and subsequently in the Peter Connelly case.

The construction of a 'full' picture by reaching a perceived 'endpoint' to jigsaw work is organisationally bounded, inevitably situated and, as the extracts in this chapter have shown, subject to ongoing revision. Public inquiry reports 'rewrite' cases that are closed, where an endpoint had previously been assumed. As argued in Chapter Three, professionals may struggle to acquire a 'full' picture of a child's circumstances because once taken out of the context in which information is offered, received and understood, the meaning of that information changes; it is actions in *context* that gives information particular meaning. The interview extracts have shown that professional references to 'pictures' or 'pieces' of a jigsaw are actions that produce versions of events for the practical purpose at hand (for example, to reach an endpoint). Thus, information is acted on at various points as 'pieces', 'snippets', 'snapshots' or 'pictures' are passed from one agency to the next. These actions are transformative, as they code and rewrite the 'nature' of the issues. As such, these co-produced pictures are always in motion, and must be translated into something that receiving agents can 'hear'. Endpoints are achieved, but these 'endpoints' are different because organisational boundaries determine when these 'endpoints' are reached – they are different for different professionals because of where those professionals are positioned in relation to information. For example, in one social worker's account, an 'endpoint' is reached at the point of corroboration and successful prosecution. However, teachers in two different extracts highlight that 'endpoints' are reached when 'pieces' of their jigsaw can be passed on. For the teacher in the first extract, this is when she considers that she has the 'right' child protection piece within her 'full' picture. The teacher in the second extract, meanwhile, requires social services to (in)validate her concerns from the 'pieces' that she is able to offer with other available 'pieces', so that a decision can then be made about whether the connected pieces warrant professional concern (i.e. if social services does nothing with the referral [No Further Action] then the professional may assume that there are no CP concerns). In other words, organisational factors such as 'hierarchy' play a role in determining a 'full picture', with social workers securing 'authority' or organisational 'entitlement' for carrying out this task. This is a fundamental point both in terms of the burden of responsibility placed at the 'front door' of children's services and also in terms of explaining why practice falls down. For example, education professionals may assume that having passed on their picture of child concerns, the receiving agency then works to finalise a picture. In reality, however, the conditions for achieving a 'full picture' in children's services referral teams can be far from conducive. Reaching an 'endpoint' in jigsaw work may have more to do with the priority or categorisation attached to incoming work in busy referral teams than any detailed qualitative observations pursued. A decision of 'no further action' firmly establishes a 'picture' of no serious concerns to a child vis-à-vis child protection, but this categorisation may be achieved as a consequence of organisational imperatives such as the management of workflow to already overstretched 'front door' social work teams (Broadhurst et al, 2010).

This chapter adds to the debate begun in previous chapters surrounding issues of complexity in information sharing. It is clearly is possible for a number of professionals to be involved in a case and still miss signs of child maltreatment, because each professional is concerned with reaching their own organisationally relevant endpoint. Once this endpoint has been reached, the case shifts into a different ontological position ('on file', 'closed' or 'monitored'), meaning that the 'full' picture cannot be carried on indefinitely. Each agency has its own jigsaw (police jigsaw, health jigsaw, school jigsaw, social work jigsaw and so on), and the different 'endpoints' required, as well as the organisational constraints of the roles of the professionals involved, will determine the work that is done with it. Context, sense making and translation all matter in determining what gets said and remains unspoken, what is passed on, how information is understood and the priority assigned to it at any point in time. Understanding these factors helps us to recognise why connections may not be made, despite failings seeming obvious in retrospect during inquiries into the circumstances surrounding child deaths. It is hoped that such understandings will help inform the serious case review process.

Professional questions for reflection

1. How does something become a 'piece' of your agency's jigsaw?
2. How do you know when certain 'pieces' fit a jigsaw?
3. How do you make sense of incoming 'pieces'?
4. Are you maintaining a focus on how you are securing connections between pieces?
5. Do you have an understanding of what 'pieces' other agencies need to compile a jigsaw?
6. At what point do you think that you have a 'full' picture?

7. At what point do you pass on your 'picture' to somebody else? What prompts you to do this? Have you checked out how the receiver understands your story and what sense they then make of it?

SEVEN

Professional relationships with information

Introduction

The interview extracts in Chapter Six highlight the joining together of information (akin to assembling a jigsaw puzzle) and explore how presumptions about 'full' pictures frame actions by professionals within different organisational settings. Relationships are central for these processes to work effectively, and it is relationships to which this chapter now turns. Relationships among professionals tasked with sharing information to safeguard children are on the one hand mandatory, and are very much viewed in inter-professional terms. Lines of accountability and obligation are written down in national and local policy documents. For example, policy guidance such as the *Working together* publications tells us that relationships between professionals is a fundamental tenet for safeguarding children, building a 'full' picture of children's lives. Performing information-related tasks to protect and promote the welfare of children becomes a very difficult pursuit if 'good' working relationships are not established. I am sure that all professionals, in whatever field, will unequivocally agree with this. However, only considering relationships between professionals within their organisational roles is far too simplistic. I beg to suggest that while relationships between professionals are clearly important, perhaps more fundamental is understanding the relationship professionals have with information that is shared by other professionals, if we are to truly understand multi-agency information-sharing practices in context. Information relationships focus on when and how information is, can and should be connected. I would argue resolutely that understanding professional relationships with information is crucial to establishing how matters can get missed or de-prioritised, and remain unconnected (meaning that the relationship with information is not achieved). Issues in information sharing, coupled with understanding relationships (which are not generally considered in child welfare literature but which this chapter addresses) go some way to explaining how it is that calls for better information-sharing practices are not wholly resolved by improving multi-professional working through actions such as, training and bringing people together, to discuss a case in the same room. This chapter will thus explore relationships in the context of safeguarding children, but essentially it seeks to chart new conceptual ground by drawing into sharp focus information relationships rather than relationships between people (embodied relationships). This is not to deny that relationships between people influence both the mandatory activity of sharing information and the task of assembling a 'full picture'. However, while (embodied) relationships between people and information relationships may appear to overlap, they are, in quite important ways, not the same thing.

The role of relationships in information sharing

Previous research and literature suggest that relationships are important to information sharing in child protection (for example, Hallett and Birchall, 1992; Reder and Duncan, 2003). This is particularly so in relation to child death inquiries. For example, issues with inter-agency relationships were identified in the Climbié case. Paediatricians and police testimonies submitted to the inquiry noted the difficulties in working with social services who were perceived to be 'aggressive' (White and Featherstone, 2005, p 214). A re-analysis of Part 8 reviews (now commonly known as serious case reviews) in Wales (Brandon et al, 1999) found that failures in communication were related to inter-personal relationships; a lack of trust and respect for other professionals' views affected how professionals within networks related to one another. Issues in how information was transferred (or not) between professionals often reflected a negativity in professional relationships. Reder and Duncan (2003) also noted that inter-personal issues featured significantly in child death inquiries and led to professionals failing to exchange significant information with each other, failing to inform other professionals about decisions that had been made, and failing to pass on relevant information or call case conferences (p 83). In a study of case conferences, McGloin and Turnbull (1986) observed lack of trust between inter-agency professionals as an obstacle to communication. However, a report on integrated working by the Children's Workforce Development Council (CWDC) in 2008 stated that 76 per cent of professionals considered that trust had been developed between multi-agency professionals as a result of improved information sharing. More recently, the Multi-agency Working and Information Sharing Project (Home Office, 2014) and the establishment of information-sharing models such as multi-agency safeguarding hubs (MASHs) across localities have achieved similar results.[1] They are built on the core principles of information sharing, joint decision making and coordinated interventions through better partnership working (Home Office, 2014).

Professionals have a mandate to work together, and as such, relationships operate on the basis of sequential interdependence through the tasks performed (in this case, the sharing of information). However, Osborne (1998) foregrounds the centrality of trust, loyalty and reciprocity in the formation of interdependent relationships; it is these components that enable collaboration to be developed and maintained. Adding to this line of argument, an alternative formulation within the literature is that of the 'voluntary' network (a network conceptualised as a large professional group made up of a number of agencies). It is suggested that voluntary networks maintain loyalty for longer periods of time (Osborne, 1998, p 309), and as such, conflicts are able to be resolved on the basis of members' concerns regarding their professional reputation (Osborne, 1998). Bob Hudson (2002) argues that the success of mandated networks depends on personal relationships, although this can lead to the development of 'insider' and 'outsider' groups, which in turn jeopardises the function of the network. Consequently, factors such as informality of personal relationships and trust in networks are viewed in a negative light by those agents excluded or marginalised from the network. Osborne (1998) therefore argues that relationships based on personal trust make it hard for those 'outsiders' to gain entry into the network, with information perceived as only being passed on between those 'inside' the network and not beyond. Little consideration is given to situations where relationships with those 'inside' the network have not been gained or have yet to be established (Osborne, 1998). This is particularly noteworthy given the changing nature of the workforce so frequently reported in children's services. However, the literature says little on how these relationships (positive and negative) work with regard to information sharing in everyday *practices*. I now turn to empirical data to illustrate findings that are somewhat congruent with literature on professional relationships. Relationships in this sense continue to be important to multi-agency working, and factors such as trust and reciprocity are vital ingredients for information exchanges. However, there is complexity in the way that matters such as trust in information sharing work on the ground.

Inter-professional and inter-personal obligations in information sharing

Information relationships can be mandatory but there is variation in their performance, which is influenced by moral, temporal and spatial positioning. This is evident in the following interview extract, in which a manager working for a non-governmental agency describes information-sharing activity in her locality:

> "I think there is some really good information-sharing practice going on, I seriously do. Some agencies are really good. Some individual social workers are really good. Some teachers are fantastic and some are not. It is a real mixed bag. From our point of view, we get on … we have good relationships with other voluntary agencies without a doubt … they are improving. We've got good relationships with agencies like

[projects]. I think we have good relationships with individual social workers and I would say that the biggest hurdle we had to face from time to time … good relationships with health … really good. They are quick to respond and they ask what we are doing and vice versa. I would say we have a mixed bag with children's services. The police are spot on. If you phone the police, you get a response. I mean, some people are precious with information. I mean, we could get a referral from a social worker and say 'Can we come and read the files?' and you get some of the 'Not really but I will have to check it out' and all that palaver. It does happen, but it is that initial resistance, and kind of vice versa. If someone wants to come and read our files, then they can come and read it. They just have to sign a confidentiality clause, that's all. Bottom line is you want children to be safe. You want them to be progressing. The Data Protection Act is there for a reason and Freedom of Information is there for a reason … but you work in the interests of the child, don't you?"

Here, the manager lists the range of professional relationships that her agency has with other agencies, and more specifically, with individual professionals within the locality. These individuals are defined by their organisational 'hats'. At the same time, the manager describes information relationships; some of these are described as 'good', implying from the outset that some information relationships (which can be with the same person in a different context) can be construed as 'bad'. She considers information relationships to be 'good' when she receives a quick response (for example, in dealings with the police), and also when agencies (such as health) ask what she perceives as being the 'right' questions, such as the nature of her agency's involvement in a case. The manager claims that this is a reciprocated behaviour, and therefore by implication suggests that such relationships have value in terms of the perceived positive information practices that are fostered through them ("good relationships with health … really good. They are quick to respond and they ask what we are doing and vice versa"). She states that information relationships are 'not good' when she is faced with resistance from individuals at the point where an information relationship is being established, for example when her agency makes a request for information. Here this relationship with information is described as 'precious', echoing notions of 'value' developed in Chapter Three. Any reluctance to share data is then situated within the legal framework of information provision (the Data Protection and Freedom of Information Acts), but is countered with what seems like an odd statement: "but you work in the interests of the child". This latter statement suggests that despite legal parameters, the manager is aware that there are other information relationships that must be invoked at times when the situation demands it, even where these might be unofficial. Nonetheless, the 'interests of the child' serve to justify evaluations of the information relationship, such that a person who withholds information can be morally censured. Inter-professional obligations in information relationships and the way in which information practices may vary between individuals is further described in the following interview extract from a Group Intervention Panel (GRIP) worker, whose role is to work with children and young people at risk of entering the youth justice system. He attributes this variation in part to his working pattern, with information relationships being affected by whether or not he is physically present in the workplace:

> "[It] can depend who you speak to with the police to be honest. Someone will act straight away with the information … on the same day, but for others, 'Oh, I will do it later' sort of thing. Sometimes you can spend all day trying to chase information but it can depend who asks for the information. Now if I ring up … 'cos I work there two days a week … I know for a fact that when I go in on the Wednesday it will be in my tray. But if someone else rings up, they will say 'I still haven't got that information' so can you chase them up … so when I go in on Wednesdays and Thursdays they will go, 'Oh, I will do it now.'" (GRIP worker)

The GRIP worker begins his account by stating that variations in information relationships arise because of the need to communicate with a range of different individuals, in this case police officers. He makes it clear that disparities in information practice relate to time issues, or to the level of responsiveness of individuals receiving requests. ("Someone will act straight away with the information … on the same day, but for others, 'Oh, I will do it later' sort of thing"). The GRIP worker describes information as something that can be 'pursued' or 'tracked down', although whether this process take place depends on who has requested the information. It is at this point that the the GRIP worker changes from the third to the first person, describing his own, rather than GRIP's, relationship to information. In doing so he makes a distinction between his relationship with information sought from the police and that of others linked to his organisation. The worker positions himself as a figure familiar to the police, being seconded (as part of his job) to the police station for two days a week. He acknowledges that he is in a privileged position by having his requests for information addressed in a timely fashion. He is also very aware that where he is physically situated for part of the week has value in terms of the immediacy placed on his requests for information; this is a recognised privilege that others do not have, as can be seen from the delayed responses they receive from the police when they request information. As such, the GRIP worker acts as a 'go-between' for others in order to speed up responses to information that they have requested.

Features of trust in information relationships

As highlighted in the introduction to this chapter, as well as in Chapter Four's discussion of the professional needs of information users, the dimension of trust has been shown to be a vital ingredient for professionals working together as well as for information sharing. The issue of trust is examined in more detail in the following interview extract from a police officer:

> "I would always question it [information]. I would always want to know more because no one ever

gives you the perfect scenario or the perfect case notes, so I would always question information that is given to me. You see a lot of information sharing is done ad hoc … or always on the phone. In this case relationships are really important because otherwise I would be guarded with information. So if a probation officer asked for information … we don't work closely with probation, as closely as we should, and equally there is a bit of reticence sometimes from probation to come on side. They are a statutory body and there are certain obligations of probation but for whatever reason they don't share information or engage with anyone. There is no professional one to one trust there … you know if we get requests for information from probation, or someone else we don't know then we [the police] would say 'Please put that request in writing for us … fax, email, and we will respond in kindness when we can.' That's how we do it with them [probation] but not others we do not have good working relationships with … it's more I scratch your back, you scratch mine type of thing … that is how it works." (Police officer)

The police officer states that he does not take his information relationships for granted, but rather questions his information sources to varying degrees. He applies this process of questioning mainly to individuals 'outside' of his agency who are unable to provide him with a 'complete' picture ("I would always want to know more because no one ever gives you the perfect scenario or the perfect case notes"). As such, he is required to build up his own 'complete' picture because there is still more out there to be known. Here, we can see echoes of the jigsaw metaphor discussed in Chapter Six. However, there is a further issue here, which is one of 'trust'. The police officer draws on the informal aspects of information exchange, which are encapsulated in the final sentence: "it's more I scratch your back, you scratch mine type of thing … that is how it works". Throughout the extract, it is clear that information exchange requires more than just lines of accountability. Accountability is not quite enough in facilitating successful information sharing; rather, it is the inter-personal, 'embodied', one-to-one relationships that matter: "relationships are really important because otherwise I would be guarded with information".

Embodied relationships in terms of knowing someone is proposed as a way of trusting the information relationship. Where embodied relationships do not exist, information relationships are distant (reflecting a lack of 'close' working) and become formalised (i.e. *'put that request in writing')*. This means that the information-sharing process takes longer, although it retains an element of generosity (*'we will respond in kindness'*). In other words, when embodied relationships are not established, formal processes for sharing and receiving information incur time delays. Although embodied relationships take time to build; there are benefits,which include reciprocity between professionals or agencies within the network (for example *'I scratch your back, you scratch mine'*). Actions of reciprocity are important in information-sharing activity, but how reciprocity works in practice is far from straightforward. For example, the police officer suggests that when professionals from probation *do* attend case conferences or other multi-agency meetings and share information, their input is received by him and others 'within' the network as being incredibly valuable. However, probation's attendance at such meetings is described as being 'sporadic'. This suggests that for informal embodied relationships to prove successful in information relationships, reciprocity must be reliable, even when it is known that information of value is there to be had. The importance of individual relationships and trust are further confirmed by a primary care trust (PCT) manager:

> "I suppose the role that I'm in I've built up key working relationships with numerous multi-agency professionals, particularly in social care, the police and probation and YOTs [youth offending teams] … it's all about trust. So I know the professionals that are phoning me with information. If I don't know somebody who is giving the information then I will phone them back, or I will say 'Who are you working with?' But because we have turnovers of staff often

their introduction to me is 'Your name has been given to me by ...' so it might be a senior manager, so that makes me feel safe that this information is probably coming from a kosher source. Although it also depends on the information that is being relayed as to whether I might think 'Perhaps this is a bit too vague and I need more information', so then I would, with my networking that I have, my source of networks, then I would start by making further enquiries. I would say ... it's quite interesting ... but it depends on the professional you are dealing with. For me the most difficult person was someone from probation who would not give me the information that was needed on a person we had in our hospital. They said 'You will need to ring the social worker who will tell you all.' That was really interesting and I said 'But why can't you share this information with me, because I need that information. I need to know this if I am setting up a risk assessment here' and the response to that was 'The social worker has all that information so you will have to get hold of them.' Now there was a time delay of two hours plus because the social worker was in fact very, very busy and out of the office at the time. So I could have set up what I needed to set up in the trust without a time delay, and so I think that was unacceptable."

Trust features heavily in the PCT manager's account. Personal networks matter, so much so that problems can emerge when personal relationships do not exist: "I had never any dealings with this probation officer before, so I just thought to myself I wonder if you actually understand my role and the reason for my request for information." Quite clearly we can assume there is no trust in this professional relationship. Most notably, however, the PCT manager adds a further dimension to trust through her narrative, which is trust in information shared. Relationships that are built up over time between individuals facilitate good information relationships that enable individuals to make judgements about the reliability of information. Information from a trusted source does not appear to require questioning or validation (because the manager knows the information provider personally, or is familiar with their agency), and therefore does not incur delay, something that was also indicated by the police officer. By contrast, a similar transaction with someone that the manager is not familiar with in itself casts doubts on the value of information being offered; the information relationship is uncertain and therefore a process of questioning and validation is required. The manager explains how these processes of questioning and validation work by describing how she telephones the agency that the source of information claims they are from, or questions the source about who they work with. It is here that a feature of trust comes into play in that it may facilitate the transfer of embodied relationships in a changing workforce: "But because we have turnovers of staff often their introduction to me is 'Your name has been given to me by …' so it might be a senior manager, so that makes me feel safe that this information is probably coming from a kosher source."

In contrast to the police officer, the manager describes trust as being something that can be transferred as well as embodied. This transferability is acknowledged by both parties in the information relationship; it is used as a resource to gain information ("'Your name has been given to me by …'") and is also used as a resource in interpreting information that is given ("it might be a senior manager so that makes me feel safe"). In other words, if during the exchange the person offering information can provide names of individuals the manager has established previous information relationships with, or they are able to provide a name that the manager recognises as part of her network, this can act as authorisation that information is something that can legitimately be given or received. However, the manager describes information as something that is owned, and something that can be held back from her, depending on who she has requested the information from. This is a problem for her as the delay caused by these transactions unduly affects her ability to carry out her role responsively. Similar to the police officer, the manager makes specific reference to an exchange with a probation officer that she has not had a previous encounter with; this is an example of one individual (defined by their organisational 'hat') who has created a problem for her ("the most difficult person was someone from probation who would not give me the information that was needed") in that information that she required to carry out her job was held back. In this case, the probation officer 'signposts' the manager to a social worker who is the professional recognised by the probation officer as *the* person holding the information that the manager requires. The information held by the social worker is seen as relevant to the manager's information needs, and therefore has value in terms of her being able to carry out her role responsively and effectively.

The accounts presented so far in this chapter exemplify that actions of information sharing have both inter-professional and inter-personal dimensions, which resonates with findings from other studies. In terms of an inter-professional dimension, we have seen that there are differences in how agencies interpret their professional obligations and organise their responses. However, inter-personal relationships are clearly important. They can facilitate or inhibit smooth information-sharing practices as well as enable judgements to be made about the reliability of information relationships, and as such they are an important resource in information sharing. I now take this chapter in a slightly different direction by drawing on observations relating to issues that are less well documented in the literature, namely information relationships and the notion of positioning to information.

Positioning and connections with information

Professionals are positioned differently in relation to information. This influences the connections they make (or not) with information they have, and the work they do with it. The main features of this context relate to information requirements and relevance. Information requirements determine what is received and what is not received. What is important at any given time, and in any given context, is not so at other times and in other contexts; the circumstances always relate to the practical purposes at hand, as described by the GRIP worker cited earlier:

"[O]n the police system it might ping up a name but they look at it from a criminal perspective because they are the police. I don't look at it like that personally. Like I say I don't really give a monkey's what the parents have done, you know. It doesn't bother me because it's the kids I am interested in. So when I go round to the house I go round with a completely blank canvas. I don't think 'Oh, he was done for assault or she has been shop lifting.' I don't look at it like that ... I don't even take them into consideration, you know because I am there for the young person ... I don't generally bother with the information if I'm honest with you."

The GRIP worker describes how professionals are positioned differently in regard to information, on account of their information requirements or relevance. His statements are particularly salient with regard to understanding information relationships, and where things can go wrong. In his role as a GRIP worker, he disregards certain kinds of information he wants no relationship with, and therefore does not do anything with it. He justifies his non-action to police information by stating his position in relation to this information ("I don't really give a monkey's what the parents have done.... It doesn't bother me because it's the kids I am interested in.... I don't really bother with the information if I'm honest with you"). Quite clearly, positioning influences relevance, as the GRIP worker is interested in a particular type of information. He prioritises information relating to the young people he works with, and not information that the police may hold on the young person's parents. However, there is a further complexity to positioning, and that is that it can be subject to change when external influences alter. The GRIP worker states that his relationships to information and his information requirements are subject to change (in that different kinds of information are prioritised depending on the circumstances), and so too is his positioning to information, as he later explains:

"Well, for instance we've got a YOT inspection on the 31st March so when the inspectors come they will log on to the system, and they will look at that … you know are your contacts up to date … like case management…. It's just you've got to log it … everything! It can be a bit of a nuisance really because the inspection that's coming up at the moment we've got to be right up to date. I was off last week so I am going to be spending the next two days on my PC from 9 o'clock making sure everything is up to date."

The GRIP worker defines the parameter for information (a YOT inspection), which demands different information requirements from those in the worker's day to day role – the inspection requires him to deprioritise information that is usually a priority for him in his daily work. Thus, for the purpose of the YOT inspection, information that the GRIP worker usually constructs as being 'background' information shifts to becoming 'foreground' information. He describes system information, making reference to different information types that place different time demands on him, and demonstrating how different repositories (such as systems, people, or forms) make different information relevant. Importantly, the GRIP worker implies that information does not have to be up to date for him to carry out his work; his day-to-day role is about other types of information (for example, as noted earlier, "it's the kids I am interested in") and not about system information, or feeding data into that system. However, for other professionals, such as social workers, keeping up-to-date system information (record keeping) is a key imperative and a key indicator measured in Ofsted inspections. Therefore, depending on the profession, the context and/or the intended point of purpose, there are different kinds of information, with different uses, relevance and values assigned to them.

Professional information needs, relevance and positioning

R (researcher): "Do you think that the information you need to identify or deal with concerns is the same for others that you work with?"

M (midwife): "Well, it would be good if we all had the same information, and have the answers in front of us as to what people are. You have your own expertise and you really identify problems and look for information that relates to that area of expertise … that is what I am here for … midwifery. In the same way I acknowledge that a health visitor would see things in a four-year-old that I might not identify as a midwife. So because of her specialisms she is more likely to identify things and want information that is relevant to her area of expertise which would not be a concern for me."

R: "OK, so do you think practices or agencies vary with regards to what information they need to identify or deal with concerns about children and families?"

M: [Long pause] "Well, I do obviously think that agencies do look at things from their own points of view, and that, and their area of specialism, determines what information is important to them and what isn't necessarily relevant … it's the same as what I have just said about health visitors and midwives. But I think that the more information you are able to share, the more likely you are of building a complete picture, and that helps all the agencies involved because we all bring our own focus to the table, so that is for whatever agency is working."

The midwife's responses provide explicit recognition that professionals have different information needs, and are positioned differently in relation to information. Perhaps more importantly, however, the midwife suggests that professionals work on the basis that there is a complete set of the 'same information or a 'complete picture'. Within her account, the midwife clearly acknowledges that different professionals do not see things in the same way, and therefore information requirements will differ depending on where the professional is positioned in relation to information. As such, organisational roles, and knowledge specific to that role, provide the parameters in which information is constructed as being relevant. A professional's positioning in relation to information means that multi-agency professionals will have different frames of sense making that will fundamentally influence the connections that are made to information, and the work that is done with it. The midwife makes it clear that information that is relevant to a health visitor will not be considered relevant to her, and thus no connection will be made between that particular type of information and what she regards as an information requirement, or information that is relevant to her in performing her role. With regard to information relevance, a housing officer makes reference to what information is relevant to him in performing his role, and articulates what he thinks is relevant to someone else:

> "I think it (the referral form) puts you off partly … it's scary, yeah. Like I say if I printed one off for you now … even sort of when you have been doing them for a while … you would see that the back two pages are not relevant to us but yet they are still there. I just feel that when I emailed that form, I didn't fill in the back two pages because I am not a healthcare professional, because I feel that is what they were asking me … health care questions, you know. They weren't relevant to me as a housing officer to answer. Why would I have health information when I am not a healthcare professional? I don't need that kind of information to do my job dealing with anti-social behaviour." (Housing officer)

The housing officer offers this account in the context of making a referral to children's services; it is in this context that he communicates expectations of filling out referral forms. It is by the action of form filling that the housing officer makes it clear that he knows what is not relevant to him, but also what he thinks is relevant to someone else, which in this case are questions relevant to healthcare professionals. The housing officer poses the question (and also by way of seeking validation) of why he would hold health information because of where he is positioned in relation to that information (under the organisational banner of 'housing'). He states that health information is not relevant to him in his organisational role, and therefore queries why health-related questions remain on a referral form that is sent to him as a housing officer, when he would not hold the information required to answer those questions. Quite clearly, we see that the housing officer does not have a relationship with that type of information. Health information is not considered an information requirement for him when dealing with housing issues under the remit of 'anti-social behaviour', and so no relationship is made. The housing officer implies that health professionals 'own' health information, and therefore they are the professionals that are able to assist in meeting children's services information requirements, constructed by the referral form. Similarly, a social work team leader clearly articulates what information is not relevant to her agency, but is relevant to other agencies within the professional network:

"I really look at what is relevant to our agency.... I close the ones [contacts] down from pupil welfare and in this case I wrote to mum ... well, the RSO [referral support officer] is saying to mum that education are not clear as to where your child is living and you have parental responsibility so can you find out where he is staying and speak to pupil welfare as to why he is not going to school. So I have not gone out and done an assessment, so I have closed it down because I think pupil welfare should have done that really. I don't think it's down to us to go round chasing children because it's an educational matter. I mean, it's like when teenagers go missing then agencies ring us. Well, I close it down because

> I see that very much as a police matter because until the child is found we can't do anything. We can't go knocking doors down. We don't have the power, do we? We can't go round looking for children … it's not our place. The police have more resources to do that." (Social work team leader)

These are the words of a social work team leader working in a frontline initial assessment team. Her account is in the context of her decision making on receiving referrals while on duty. She makes reference to information that is organisationally relevant to her agency, and closing information that she feels is more relevant to other agencies. As such, she makes it clear that a process of ordering takes place when she acquires information. In other words, there is a professional hierarchy, or an assumed allocation of who should get what information, and who should act on that information: "So I have not gone out and done an assessment, so I closed it down because I think pupil welfare should have done that really." Although the social work team leader clearly allocates which professionals should be acquiring which information and acting on that information, it remains unclear as to whether this information ordering is shared across all individuals, agents and agencies across the locality research site. This question could also be asked of localities more generally, both nationally and internationally in Anglophone countries. Not knowing such has proved to have serious implications, as evident in the Peter Connelly case in which the child's GP had concerns about Peter but had assumed that someone else who was better placed would act on that information. A mandated network of professionals all making the fallible assumption that someone else will act may result in no action being taken, and thus it is imperative that information ordering is made explicit to all those within the network.

Conclusion

In policies and guidance for professionals responsible for safeguarding children, 'interpersonal relationships' and 'information relationships' are often seen in parallel rather than being ontologically different, and as such the complexity of how these relationships work in situated information-sharing practices is rarely revealed. Embodied and information relationships add another dimension to professionals' mandate to work together in the name of child welfare and protection. Such relationships must be taken into account, alongside government policy and procedure for working together and sharing information, to fully understand the complexity of information-sharing activity. As interview extracts in this chapter, as well as in Chapters Five and Six, show, professionals in the main adhere to the policy guidance. The interviews also show that all relationships in information-sharing practice are socially organised, and, perhaps more importantly, that there are formal and informal logics of information sharing. These have been explored here in more detail, and in doing so, the chapter has drawn out a distinction between interpersonal and inter-professional relationships and professional relationships with information. Data examples presented in this chapter have shown that all relationships in information sharing practices are socially organised, but perhaps more importantly they have shown that there are formal and informal logics of information sharing, which have been explored in detail. In doing so, this chapter has drawn out a distinction between interpersonal and inter-professional relationships and professional relationships with information. Supporting findings from earlier studies, the examples in this chapter have clearly shown that embodied relationships (between people) are very important for information-sharing practices.

There are a number of features of embodied relationships that have been drawn out of the professionals' accounts in this chapter. The first feature is that embodied relationships extend to agency roles, as highlighted by the NGO manager ("the police are spot on, there is a bit of reticence sometimes from probation to come on side"; "good relationships with health"). As such, 'good' relationships on an agency level can translate to 'good' relationships with individual professionals and vice versa. However, the moral quality assigned to agency and individual relationships ('good' or 'bad') derives from information relationships, situated in and changing across time and place, that can facilitate or inhibit smooth information-sharing transactions.

A second feature of embodied relationships is 'validation', which is clearly illustrated by the police officer and the PCT manager. Validation is a feature that distinguishes between formal and informal information-sharing practices. As explained earlier in this chapter, informal information exchanges often take place over the telephone and lead to a speedy response. As suggested by Osborne (1998), the informality of relationships means that information is often passed on between those within the network. This has consequences for those who have not established embodied relationships, particularly in a changing workforce. However, formal information exchanges require more effort for both parties (on the part of the person requesting information and for the person responding to the request). This leads to a time delay in responding, which consequently slows down the transaction. Such formal processes (such as written requests for information) occur when a professional or agency is unsure about the status or affiliation of the individual making the information request. This is seen in the police officer's reluctance to share information over the phone in the absence of an established relationship with the individual he is speaking to. These differentials imply that despite professionals having a mandate to share information, the process that follows rests on the moral quality of embodied relationships, and thus the experience, rather than being standardised, will be different for everyone, or each agency, within the locality network.

Reciprocity and trust are also features of embodied relationships, although these are not straightforward. For informal embodied relationships to be successful, reciprocity between agencies must be reliable and not sporadic, even if the information to be had is regarded as valuable. Trust, and the way in which it works, is not straightforward. Early work by Hallett and Birchall (1992) argues that the notion of trust within relationships has become tautological (for individuals to trust each other, it is important to develop trusting relationships), providing little empirical evidence of how trust relationships actually work in practice. This chapter challenges this view through its offering of a variety of narrative accounts that demonstrate that the complexity in the way that trust works in practice – professionals' knowledge of their fellow professionals – is a key resource. It is an aid to sense making in terms of judging the reliability of information and in terms of tacit expectations (that is, reciprocation). This encourages the flow of information relationships by speeding things up and getting individuals to go the 'extra mile'. Trust can be seen as something that is not only embodied but something that can be transferred, as highlighted by the PCT manager. A lack of trust requires more work in that the information relationship is uncertain and validation is required for both the source of information and the quality of the information that is being offered. The transferability of trust is something that is acknowledged as possible by parties to information relationships where previous information relationships have been secured.

The second part of this chapter concerns positioning and how information is socially organised. The interview extracts indicate how professionals are positioned differently to information, and have different information requirements that are defined by very practical purposes; organisational boundaries mark out what information is relevant, or what is considered as being valuable to meet information requirements. This influences the relationships people have with information, the connections that people make and the work they do with information. The interviews show that professionals recognise that they are positioned differently to information, recognise other professionals' position to information in relation to their own, and have different relationships to information as a result of this. It is here that the issue of relevance is made clear. However, another important feature in relation to positioning to information is the quality attributed to information. The NGO manager in attributes 'vagueness' to the quality of information that she receives; she is expressing this from a specific position, although this view may not be shared with others who are positioned differently in relation to that information, and may consider it to wholly adequate or informative. Thus, it is not just relationships between people that are important, but professional relationships to information in terms of the respective practical purposes that present themselves. However, it is important to note at this point that relationships to information are not static but are subject to change depending on the task at hand. This was clearly manifest in the GRIP worker's account where a YOT inspection provided the parameters of information, and meant that the information he prioritised in this context was different from the information requirements he prioritised in his daily work and which were considered important to his role. Thus, information relationships are not just organisationally bounded, but are subject to change within specific contexts in which information changes meaning and action (as discussed in more detail in Chapter Three).

The fluidity of professional relationships to information has been seen in this chapter to be influenced by the form that information takes. The form that is taken is influenced by the embodiment of professional relationships, and the features that these encompass, as discussed earlier in this chapter. As the extract from the police officer's interview shows, the perceived nature of the police–probation relationship, and police perceptions of probation not fulfilling their statutory obligations in engaging with other professionals or taking part in information-sharing activity in the main, means that the police adopt a formal medium in their information exchanges with the probation service. The police officer highlights that information is something that can be given or requested, and suggests that a formal response to requests for information are adopted with probation ("please put the request in writing for us ... fax ... email") as well as with people that he is unfamiliar with. Time becomes a factor in this; there is no urgency in dealing with requests for information that follow this route ("we will respond in kindness when we can"). This may be construed as creating what Hudson (2002) terms as 'insider' and 'outsider' groups, suggesting that these group divisions have the potential to jeopardise the function of a professional network. Within the confines of this research, probation services may therefore be considered by the police as an 'outsider' group because of their failure to 'play' the information-sharing 'game' like everybody else. Reder and Duncan (2003) suggest that those deemed 'outsiders' may be kept at a distance through minimal interaction, which is fuelled by the negative perceptions of the 'insiders' (p 92). By implication, this has consequences and may limit what can be known about a child and their family, particularly where there is valuable or critical information held by probation to be had. Unfortunately, no probation officers took part in this research, so their views cannot be reflected here.

Formal responses for sharing information are more time consuming and labour intensive than their informal counterpart. For the police, informal information-sharing practices take the form of telephone exchanges ("done ad hoc on the phone") and are based on the moral quality of working relationships. In this way, and perhaps importantly, information is conveyed orally, and therefore may be considered as embodied. However, the formal medium of information exchange (requests for information in writing) is disembodied, which alters the relationship that professionals have with information. Put another way, information in a written form detaches information from the body and is reformulated into something that the receiver relates to in a different way. Considered in this way, the receiver can reflect on the information at leisure, and without the presence of the source, and this alters not only the relationship to information, but also the meaning of the information that is exchanged. Serious consideration needs to be given to embodied and disembodied information flows, as different kinds of information exchange (sending or receiving a fax, face-to-face encounters in a meeting, emails, conversations in the car, and so forth) will alter a professional's relationship to that information through the context in which it is offered and understood. Consequently, the form of the exchange will affect how information is interpreted and ultimately the meaning that is assigned.

Taking the research findings presented here collectively, this chapter has, in a small way, contributed to understanding some of the complexities that are present in mandated networks of people tasked with sharing information. In looking beneath the rhetoric of 'working together', professional narratives in this chapter again show that information sharing in multi-agency settings remains something that is not easily resolved. It has to be worked at, and this raises a number of important questions. Is it a straightforward matter of encouraging better relationships between individuals, improving processes, protocols and legislation? What is it about relationships that improve information sharing? Empirical data coupled with these questions challenges some of the assumptions underlying the call for improved relationships in information sharing that largely remain taken for granted.

Managers' questions for reflection

1. How are positive relationships fostered at executive levels? How is trust built in your agency, and how is this trust transferred to all levels of the organisation (not just in terms of what constitutes individual roles but in the way that managers trust one another)?

2. Is the ordering of information (that is, what information belongs to whom, and who should act on what information) shared across all locality frontline professionals (including managers) and agencies? How do you ensure that this information is shared, particularly in the context of a changing workforce?

3. What contexts or locality events can be created to promote or establish positive working relationships within and between agencies in which trust can be engendered? How can this be featured into multi-agency safeguarding hub (MASH) arrangements? Is this something that could be incorporated into induction training, or similar, for new workers joining your agency?

Professional questions for reflection

1. Why are relationships important in information sharing? What are the important qualities that professionals could work on, for example, consistency, predictability, reciprocity, validation?

2. It might help with question 1 to ask who you have your best relationships with. Why is this? How do they work (for example, how often do you see each other and so on)?

3. Have you ever passed on information to someone you trust and been upset/angry or disagreed with what they did with that information? How has this experience affected your subsequent working relationship with them?

4. Is the allocation of who has what information, and who should act on that information, shared by those in your agency? How do you know this?

Note

[1] MASH models are multi-agency safeguarding hubs/models aimed at improving information sharing and local safeguarding responses through arrangements such as the co-location of professionals including the local authority, police, health, probation and so forth.

EIGHT

Emotion information: working with hunches, concerns and uncertainty

Introduction

> "Part of me, with the feelings I got from the visit with mum, it must have been something that was still niggling me and I suggested just to be on the safe side, just to be certain, just to make sure, that she was not returned to Manning's." (Senior professional in Haringey, cited in Laming, 2003, p 187)

In the previous chapter, professional narratives demonstrated how information relationships and inter-personal relationships are central in professionals' work of safeguarding children. The very nature of child protection work means that it is relationship-based, reinforced by the mandate of 'working together' in which epistemologies of welfare, health, education, and law converge. However, there is an emotional dimension to child protection work that is highlighted very clearly in the opening quote from a senior social worker in Haringey, taken from the inquiry into the death of Victoria Climbié in February 2000. The social worker discusses a 'niggling' feeling about Victoria's situation and her potential return to the family home where Victoria lived with her aunt and her aunt's boyfriend, Carl Manning. Quite clearly we can infer that the senior practitioner was working from an emotional response that was difficult to define and set down in terms of 'evidence'. Despite important 'emotional signals' such as those highlighted here, the emotional and relational aspects of social work practice have become increasingly marginalised (Morrison, 2007), with emotions only discussed in theoretical terms within the field of social work (Taylor and White, 2001 ;Cooper, 2005; Ferguson, 2007; Morrison, 2007). Arguably, a drive towards evidence-based practice has meant that feelings are not considered sufficient grounds on which to act, despite feelings being both an important source of information for the worker, and a trigger for action, as indicated in the Laming report (Laming, 2003) and the Munro review (Munro, 2011).

Information at the level of 'feeling', and what people do as a result of feelings, is increasingly lost through 'technical-rational' responses (Schon, 1983) that favour notions of 'objectivity' and 'reason'. Wastell and colleagues (2010) point out that this can have unintended effects where practice becomes habitualised in meeting performance targets rather than the 'proper' work of social work. In a Radio 4 Today programme in 2008, referring to the death of 17-month-old Peter Connelly and to the managerial focus pertaining to the case, Munro explained that 'Haringey had a beautiful paper trail of how they failed to protect this baby'. Quintessentially, while there are references to emotions in the inquiry report into Peter Connelly's death, there is no analysis of their significance in terms of what information is shared and how, and the decisions that are subsequently made. 'Rational' and emotional approaches to social work are often seen in binary opposition, with rational approaches increasingly regarded as having the monopoly as an effective means to manage risk (Taylor and White, 2001). Taylor and White (2001) further suggest that: 'Emotions are not the messy and recalcitrant enemies of rationality, but are absolutely integral to the processes of decision-making and judgement' (p 52).

There is a significant body of literature identifying that emotion is relevant to child protection; examples include the emotional realities of child protection work (Cooper, 2005); the emotional politics of child protection work (Warner, 2015); the emotions and psycho-social dynamics of child protection (Ferguson, 2007); coping strategies in relation to child protection work (Anderson, 2000) refocusing supervision in frontline social work (Gibb, 2001); emotional intelligence in social work practice (Morrison, 2007); and empirical work on the social construction of emotions in child protection work in Norway, analysed in professional case talk (Forsberg and Vagli, 2006). Despite this, there has been relatively little empirical analysis of emotions in everyday child protection work. More specifically, there is a significant dearth of empirical analysis of the relationship between the role of emotions and information sharing. Reder and Duncan's commentary on serious case reviews (2003) raises some important questions regarding 'communication' and 'emotion', but these questions have not been subject to any detailed research analysis. Andrew Cooper (2005) has previously called for policy analysis that is better grounded in recognition of the emotional needs of professionals and their organisations. Little had changed in regard to this until the reawakening of emotions in child protection work by Eileen Munro and her review of child protection in 2011. Firmly articulated in Munro's recommendations for a 'roll-back' of guidance and proscription and a 'roll-out' of a greater degree of flexibility, is the role of emotion, including 'the professional capacity to reflect on and manage emotions' (Munro, 2011, p 25, para 2.7):

'The assumption that records provide an adequate account of a helping profession has led to a distortion of the priorities of practice. The emotional dimensions and intellectual nuances of reasoning are undervalued in comparison with simple data about service processes such as time to complete a form.' (Munro, 2011, p 20, para 1.19)

As the Munro report acknowledges, professionals need to (be helped to) manage their emotions to reduce the risk of distorted reasoning. They also need to acknowledge and manage the role emotions play in information exchange and recording – not only as a means of potential distortion, but also as a means of understanding situations (Damasio, 1994). This is not simply a question of talking about 'white noise' being excluded (Luhmann, 1995).

This chapter now turns to an empirical analysis of professionals' emotions and feelings in respect of information sharing. Chapter Two showed how information-sharing guidance foregrounds 'purpose' with regard to how the institutionalised activity of 'information sharing' should be operationalised in professional practice; this is made visually apparent in the most recent information-sharing advice for practitioners (HM Government, 2015a, 2015b). Chapter Four, however, presented an alternative model of 'information behaviour' proposed by Wilson (1981), foregrounding 'needs' of information users that prompt different information-related behaviours. Returning to this theme, this chapter explores the relationship between what I refer to as 'emotion information' and information behaviour, by drawing on various professional accounts of uncertain feelings or concerns, and showing how such concerns then drive or affect information behaviour. In this respect, I will show that emotion information can be central to information sharing, in that it can act as a driver for other information-related behaviours where professionals carry out the added *emotional* burden of child protection work. However, as will become apparent, emotion information is problematic, as it is something that is not easily passed on. As a result, further work in 'translation' is needed to transform emotion information into something 'sharable' with other professionals. The 'rewriting' of emotion information leads to further complication of 'translation' and 'interpretation' on the part of the receiver, as this chapter reveals.

Emotions as action: working with 'iffy' feelings

Congruent with the literature, child protection concerns can be experienced at the level of 'feeling'. A further feature highlighted by the professional narratives in this research, however, suggests that ambiguity and uncertain feelings are 'emotion information' that can drive information behaviour. This may include investigative work with other agencies, as the manager of a non-governmental organisation (NGO) explains:

> "If there was a slight concern … if a member of staff came to me and said 'I've got an iffy feeling about so and so', through case management and supervision, we would identify if there is anyone else that we could get more information from, so say it was the

teen parent one, so obviously you would say 'Have you contacted the health visitor?' So they would then contact the health visitor to see if there was any more information. Obviously now CAF [Common Assessment Framework], now CAF is coming out, 'cos that is the whole point. We do a lot of CAFs here, so that is ideal because it saves all the ringing up."

The manager describes a member of her staff approaching her about an 'iffy feeling' concerning a child. Of significant importance here is that child protection concerns are described in terms of *feelings*. As the extract unfolds, we see that 'iffy feelings' are part and parcel of everyday routine, and, importantly, that they drive action. Cases are reported to her in her managerial role, and this sets in motion a whole host of subsequent actions. Feelings about children are not necessarily accompanied by other evidence causing concern, which is when investigative work becomes perhaps even more important, as the following extract from a primary school teacher shows:

"Sometimes you have a real feeling that something is not right. Sometimes it is an instinct where you know it is not right. Sometimes it is obvious by the way that they look and all the rest of it but it's a look in their [child's] face, they are frightened or they are upset a lot, or they are clingy but they are not allowed to tell you, so you have to do your own research to find out what is going on – a lot of this stuff is emotional." (Primary school teacher)

From her observations of a child, the teacher has 'an instinct' that something is 'not right'. Similar to the NGO manager, the teacher seeks to resolve her feelings through further actions of investigative work, in the form of doing her 'own research'. Here, we gain a sense of the teachers 'assessment' work, drawing on 'instinct' as emotion information that supported by some ambiguous aspects of the child's presentation at school. Emotion information experienced through 'instinct' is also shared by an education welfare officer (EWO), who describes how organisational constraints make it difficult to pass on such information:

> "I don't think you know [if a child is being abused] but you look at everything. You need some sort of relationship with the parent and mostly they are OK. Sometimes they are horrible but mostly they are OK. It is gut instinct that you know things are not right. You tend to notice things more if you go on instinct, but no one takes notice of that. It's difficult on a first visit unless it's really horrendous but you do come across things, and parents will let things out over a while and you think. They won't tell you everything for a start but you will have a feeling that things are not right even before they will let things out, over after a while. So if a house is incredible dirty, that is one way where it is enough that you will look at doing a referral to social services, you know."

Instinct is again central to the worker's assessment of the case, and her sense of things being 'not right'. As with the teacher, the EWO illustrates that 'gut instinct' (a term that has an essentialist quality, something akin to 'innate' feelings) guides the sense that is made of what is observed. However, there is a further matter brought to the fore. The EWO clearly describes that 'gut instinct' is not something that is easily dealt with in professional work ("but no one takes notice of that"); rather, the worker needs to find something more tangible, if she wants to pass the case on to social services ("So if a house is incredible dirty, that is one way where it is *enough* that you will look at doing a referral to social services, you know" – emphasis added). Here we can see that feelings are not sufficient grounds on which to act (Cooper, 2005), but can drive the worker to identify something more concrete on which to pin her emotion information; in the extract, the example given is a house that is 'incredibly dirty'. Incidentally, what the worker is doing here is 'translating' her feelings into something more substantive, seeking to support emotion information with other information that is 'enough' to make her emotion information referable. Put succinctly, emotion information is often present at the boundary of referral making or information sharing, but is not easily 'passed on'. In order to address emotion information by making a referral, it must be 'translated' into something non-emotional (such as a dirty house) that is organisationally relevant. Importantly then, translation work performed by professionals is an action that attempts to 'fill in' the gaps between what is felt, what is observed or is observable, and what actions are taken. Further acknowledging organisational constraints in terms of what can be written down in order to pass something on as a referral is articulated in the following narrative account provided by a deputy head teacher:

> "We have this tiny snippet of information but you don't know what is going to happen to that child when they go home. How is the child going to feel? What is going to happen to them? The thing is you just don't know, and that is when we need to talk to them [social services] to find out the best way for dealing with that. Sometimes there isn't the time and resources to do that properly ... in fact that is most of the time. Sometimes I think honestly with hand on my heart 'How can I send this child home to this situation? I can't do it.' Sometimes I go home and I can't sleep, thinking should I have done that or should I have done the other, but how can you write those feelings down on a referral, when quite often you make a referral and you don't even get a response back." (Secondary school deputy head teacher)

The teacher's account describes the difficulty of passing on a 'feeling' that, in organisational terms, is not legitimised information. The teacher has a choice in terms of holding on to her anxieties or 'translating' her anxieties into a concern that social services will (now) accept, albeit often addressed in the way she would like ("when quite often you make a referral, and you don't even get a response back"). Importantly, in the teacher's account, we can see information sharing as not only an organisational task, but also as one of emotional labour.

Emotion, translation and preserving relationships with families

Emotion information can influence professionals' information-related behaviours in other ways that are less obvious. In the following extract, a family support worker describes how workers in her agency 'talk down' concerns in order to preserve the working relationship with families:

> "Practice is that the family get a copy of the recordings that you take, and they are asked to read and sign them, which is good practice because, but I think, in turn, it has limited people's honesty, particularly in the contact sessions. I think family workers weren't honest once we knew that families were going to start reading them. They were worried how this would affect the working relationship. I think the downside to that is that the social workers were doing their work into the families and there was a lot of negativity but this wasn't being backed up in court because when they were coming into contact it was written that it was always 'rosy in the garden'. Depending on the member of staff, records are not a true reflection of what's going on. I mean, with the more experienced, perhaps there is less anxiety about the response of the parents. I think it's about confidence really, and your ability in the written word because you are writing down about things, and it's very easy to overlook something, like inclination – how do you write about inclination? In contact it can be a sharp look which sends a message to that child, and unless you are very eloquent in your writing it is very hard to write that down. If you are writing about someone, say in a contact session, so say the greeting, a greeting can be warm, and a greeting can be a greeting but it can be very cold, and non-committal, can't it? You can say [pitch raises] 'Hiya' but then you

can say [pitch lowered] 'Hiya' [sighs] – how do you write about that? Do you see what I mean? How do you truly reflect how an expression truly makes someone, or you, feel, which is important when you know that it will be shared with other people?"

The family support worker describes one way in which emotion information shapes information practices. More specifically, the extract shows how what is observed is consciously re-depicted, pre-empting consequences on relationships. The worker describes recording practices in her agency, and how contact sessions may not be recorded 'accurately' ("records are not a true reflection of what's going on") because of families' right to access to their records ("I think family workers weren't honest once we knew that families were going to start reading them"). She expresses other workers' feelings of 'worry' and 'anxiety' in jeopardising their working relationships with families, and therefore limiting the information shared. As a basis for this, the worker suggests that 'inconsistent pictures' can be generated by professionals who do not support one another's versions of the family in settings that are crucial for ensuring a child's safety (that is, in court). Court as a particular information ground, and as an arena that shapes information-related behaviours in particular ways, is described by a second family support worker as follows:

"I know some social workers, and some from our legal team who have commented, and not a lot of people would admit this, they have commented that workers tend not to write what I write in my CA2s [core assessments] because they are too scared to get it cross examined in court. So those CA2s that they are producing that end up in the court bundle, they are not going to make a shit's worth of difference to a case because the worker has been too scared to write exactly what is happening. So every now and then when they get a worker who will go out on a limb and say that did happen. I mean, you know when you are writing it you are going to have to go to court, I don't want to but I'm going to have to go. So you see there is no consistency in relation to recording." (Family support worker 2)

As with the first family support worker's account, this extract highlights how what is seen is 'talked down' in the agency. The family support worker offers the expression 'scared' to explain why some workers do not record "exactly what is happening", although she clearly states that this is not the case for her. The interviewee concludes that there is no consistency in recording practices in her agency, and that this variability reflects the level of confidence displayed by individual workers in acting on what they 'know' has happened. The descriptions provided by the family support workers may be likened to what Cohen (2001) terms 'the complex obstacles between information and action' (p 295), in that 'it is one thing to know something, and another to act on that knowledge' (Ferguson, 2007, p 785). However, the family support workers both suggest that anxiety surrounding honest reporting is potentially reduced with greater work experience in the field and with 'confidence' in one's writing ability. The first family support worker highlights the need to present emotion information in a written form to make it recognisable. However, she makes it clear that there is a difficulty in being able to capture feelings and put them into words that can be passed on. Here we can see how sense making operates on an emotional level and is therefore difficult to pass on; emotion information is 'noise' in Luhmann's sense when it comes to communication at the organisational level. Furthermore, information practices are socially organised in ways that are not recognised in official guidance so as to minimise fear, avoid scrutiny and so forth. These micro details of practice hold great significance for those working with children. Emotions are important information. The difficulty in expressing emotions, or minimising their importance, affects the sense made of received information, and explains why things are left unspoken, get missed or are de-prioritised.

Emotion and sense making

So far we have seen that feelings are a driver for (what Wilson would term) information-seeking behaviour. Feelings can, however, also be integral to information-receiving behaviour, as this generic health visitor notes:

> "I don't always accept information readily. I mean, I accept it at face value but unfortunately, you know, because of where I am based and the families that I work with, you get people saying all sorts of things. If I had a gut feeling that what anyone was saying to me was true, and it was something that I needed to be concerned about, then I would discuss this with the family myself. I mean, that becomes an issue when whoever is passing on information wants to remain anonymous. I mean, sometimes I have to say to people 'Look if you are concerned about that and it is something you have witnessed then you contact social services and pass that information on yourself', but obviously in an incident where I have felt that 'Yeah, I believe that', then it is something that I will investigate myself."

The health visitor details how a 'gut feeling' is important in shaping the sense made of information that is communicated to her (in this case, whether she deems their account of the family she works with to be truthful or not), and, importantly, the action that she then takes. In particular, 'gut feeling' is central to her distinguishing between what she does and does not need to take action on herself. Emotion here is highly relevant to what work is done with information, in terms of what is prioritised, what is filtered out, and so forth. My own non-participant observation field notes share similar reflections:

> A common issue in the department is professionals being presented with very little, or scant information from referrers. Today I asked the team leader how she managed in making a decision with very little

information, or when cases appeared ambiguous or complex. She said that if she has any doubts, or is uncertain about a case then she would carry out an initial assessment to make sure, although she says that 'gut instinct' plays a big part' in guiding the decisions that she makes every day. The team leader continued by saying that 'I use gut instinct every time for deciding what I need to do ... that is one of the best tools you've got to work with'. I asked her how long she had been in her post (which when I initially came back to my desk to write this down I thought 'well this is a bit random, or is it down to instinct that I asked it?') and she replied that she had been in the post for 6 years. There is something about professionals drawing on 'instincts' in their work – this seems particularly so in relation to decision making – I have heard the term 'gut instinct' or professionals saying 'I've got this feeling' a number of times – in general informal chats with one another, which make me think this is a significant but taken for granted aspect of practice. It seems to me that it is those professionals that have experience under their belt, or in positions that are required to make difficult calls very quickly on a daily basis, who talk more openly about using 'gut instincts' in assessing what should be done next. I do think there is something about 'instincts' or some sort of feeling that professionals get which comes with experience of practice, and levels of responsibility – this I think may be important but I am not entirely sure yet ('Bank this for later'). Is this an important observation? – I don't know, but perhaps instinct will 'call me' from beneath the depths of my consciousness and let me know whether I need to think about this a bit more! (Observation field notes, August 2007)

This excerpt is taken from early field notes while observing a children's services referral and assessment team. Early observations within the team suggested a central role played by 'gut instincts' in a team leader's decision making at the contact stage of the referral process. These feelings are used as an 'advisory tool' and are part of everyday/routine actions, reflecting the experience of other professionals quoted in this chapter. The extract shows that feelings carry important information that is used to guide or feed into the decisions (Damasio, 1994) that the team leader is required to make on incoming information; this is in how contacts made to the referral and assessment team are made sense of, and responded to. The term 'gut instinct' was used frequently (both in the field note observations and in the interviews presented in this chapter); in conversations with social workers who had been allocated cases, senior professionals or team leaders would openly say things like 'I have got a gut feeling about this one' or 'A feeling is telling me that there is something amiss here – I think we need to go out on this one ... see what you think.' These 'instincts' or 'feelings' were often expressed by 'experienced' professionals as a means to rationalise their decision making, including in post-referral work, after carrying out an initial assessment, for example. Social workers in senior positions with more work experience were more confident in drawing on and sharing those feelings with others than those with less experience. Most notably, however, other professionals (those outside of social work in children's services) do not appear to consider emotional information sufficient for making a referral to children's services, indicating a disjuncture between their perceptions of what makes legitimate referral information (valued sufficient to 'give') and those of the social workers who receive emotion information who do seem to value it in their own practices.

Emotion and 'anticipatories' of what 'might' happen

The teacher quoted earlier expressed her anticipation of what *might* happen to a child when they go home, and the significant anxieties that this creates for her. The following extract from a second EWO further illustrates how feelings can drive imagination of what might happen, or what I term 'anticipatory' information ('anticipatories'):

"I had a lot of concerns about that family … it was just a feeling I got. These were child protection concerns … I mean a feeling that K was abusing grandad, because a 12-year-old should not be in that situation basically, erm, and have you ever worked with anyone with dementia, very frustrating they can be. And as a 12-year-old when he is pushing her, I could see her pushing him, and if that happened to be at the top of the stairs. I would worry about the repercussions if I didn't refer that to social services. I think in that particular case K was not being looked after by her grandad. She effectively was the carer and she was far too young for the responsibility, and also it meant that her future was going to be seriously curtailed because she wasn't attending school, and she was becoming more and more frustrated by what was happening at home, you know it wasn't right, and it was a very difficult situation that her mother who was a chaotic drug user and was around grandad looking for money." (EWO 2)

Similar to the NGO manager, this EWO expresses child protection concerns as feelings, but these feelings have a further dimension in that they are underpinned by 'anticipatories' or 'imaginaries' of what might happen ("pushing him … and if that happened to be at the top of the stairs"). This influences the sense the EWO makes of the presenting case and the action she takes, which, in the example provided, is to pass on her 'anticipatories' to social services. The worker expresses feelings of 'worry' about holding on to what she thinks might happen, and the 'repercussions' of not passing on her feelings to social services. Thus, the act of passing on what she thinks *could* happen to K is a means to manage her feelings. In another example, a health service manager expressed feelings triggered by 'anticipatories' of 'what could happen' to a child when asked what she thought would happen if she did not refer the case examples given earlier in her interview account to social services:

"Then she could possibly slip through the net. She could go on to have this baby and something seriously damning could happen to this baby, and it's about accountability as well, and a duty of care. So that midwife or that professional's practice might be called into question, and we could worryingly end up going down the road of a serious case review if something untoward happened a bit further on once that baby is born. But I think generally we tend to probably over-refer but I think it's staff understanding, and cases that are not always clear." (Health service manager)

The health service manager highlights how emotion information is driven by her imagination of what might happen, which in this extract is described in terms disaster and possible child death. Her anxieties drive her action of sharing information, in the form of a referral, with social services, as implied by her suggestion that making a referral is more frequent than is always deemed necessary. However, she maximises the impact of what she is saying by constructing worst-case scenarios ("She could go on to have this baby and something seriously damning could happen to this baby... we could worryingly end up going down the road of a serious case review if something untoward happened a bit further on once that baby is born"). Pomerantz (1986) notes that 'extreme case formulations', such as this manager has articulated, may be invoked as a defensive response to perceptions of possibly being challenged. It may be construed that the manager is justifying her emotional driver to share information when the emotion information she is sharing may be open to questioning, especially as her action is based on speculative imaginaries, rather than an offering firmly indicative of harm to the baby. Thus, the 'assessment', or sense made in this case, and the action of sharing information, is temporally situated in the future, and not in the here and now. This way of working has clear implications for children's services, in that the emotional quality of information sharing broadens professional accountability, and places greater demand and a burden of responsibility at the 'front door' of children's services. Another example of this way of working can be seen in the following extract from a social worker from a non-governmental organisation, who articulates how 'worry' about what may happen to a child in the future is a driver for sharing information with local authority children's services:

> "What we have is a system where when a case is finalised we will archive them, and it will be recorded where they are archived, so they will all be kept in that sense. And again it's the appropriateness of the information so say if someone rings up and said 'I've got a funny feeling about this bloke – I want to share that information.' It may be that that information is not shared at that point, but it maybe that if that person is at significant risk then I would really worry that if we didn't share this information then it may put this child at further risk, you know, and so we would share that information [with social services] then." (Social worker, NGO)

Here, the social worker makes reference to a person outside of his agency passing on a 'funny feeling' to his agency. It is not clear whether the giver of this information is a professional or another party. Nevertheless, the social worker suggests that another person's 'undefined feeling' may not warrant sharing with anyone else at this point (currency that may be banked for later, as shown in Chapter Three), although this would depend on the perceived organisational relevance of what is being shared. Coupled with the appropriateness of the information, the catalyst that prompts him or his agency to share the described undefined feeling with social services is based on the affective feelings of worry that are experienced. What is illustrated here is that emotion information can provide both a means to secure the meaning of other types of information and the motivation for action such as information sharing.

Conclusion

There are many examples of research into the emotional aspects of child protection work. Morrison (1996) describes anxiety 'like a vein which runs through the child protection process' (p 131). Picard (2000) argues that emotion are a crucial element in individual experience and interaction with the world, and has a vital role to play in information systems, as clearly shown by social workers' comments from my observations. Irrespective of this, there has been little discussion of emotions in respect of information sharing in child protection. Thus, this chapter has focused on emotions specifically in relation to information practices, and has drawn out some very fundamental observations. Siegel (1999) states that 'emotions are more than feelings', and I would agree with this; emotions are action. This chapter has shown that emotion information (instinct, anxiety, fear and so forth) can prompt different information-related behaviours, such as making a referral to children's services. Furthermore, this chapter has shown that feelings shape information practices in many ways, such as how feelings are 'translated' into something that can be passed on; how they can influence the meaning secured to information, what is recorded, what is left unspoken and so forth. As such, information practices are socially organised in ways that are not obvious from official policy guidance.

Information-sharing guidance such as *Information sharing: Advice for practitioners providing safeguarding services to children, young people, parents and carers* (HM Government, 2015b), along with all versions of the *Working together* document, and *What to do if you are worried a child is being abused* (HM Government, 2015c), focuses on confidentiality, evidence and 'reasonable suspicion', but does not mention 'feelings', 'anxiety' or other aspects of emotion information at all. Policy guidance and procedures are 'surface instruments' (Cooper, 2005, p 4) and are useful insofar as they can guide and organise professional work. They are, however, limited in terms of addressing the deeper emotional and ambiguous realties that confront frontline professionals tasked with safeguarding children. Importantly, and as shown in the information-sharing flowchart in Chapter Two, government guidance merely posits a 'not sure' option for professionals regarding information sharing when they have concerns or feelings that cannot be defined. This can be taken as recognition of the fact that the options available to professionals are equivocal, as decision making will always involve choices, and are subject to negotiation, agreement or disagreement. However, this chapter has shown that emotions add a further dimension to the complexity of the information-sharing task. This may go some way further to explaining why information practices may not work in the ways that are intended by policymakers or why they may not be the remedial solution in extreme cases that retrospective inquiry reports suggest they should be. In respect of practice, for example, if anxieties (emotion information) are not reflected in referral information, they may not be adequately addressed, or addressed in the way that referrers would like, explaining why re-referrals rates are high. To put this in context, in the years 2013–14, 657,800 referrals were made to children's services in the UK. In 2012–13 a quarter of all referrals in England and 27% of referrals in Wales were re-referrals (NSPCC, 2015).

This chapter has also shown that emotion information is important to professionals, playing an 'advisory' role in sense making and information assessment, and driving the action of information sharing with other agencies such as children's services. As a basis for decision making, feelings may be inaccurate, or remain speculative so that no further action is taken. Cases that do not invoke powerful emotion information to drive professional action may explain in part how things get missed, remain unconnected or are not acted on. Building on findings in Chapter Seven, the current chapter shows that the role and influence of emotion information (as well as its relevance) may explain why relationships are not established with particular types of information. It also helps explains why meaning is not attributed, or connections not made, to a certain 'piece' or 'pieces' of the jigsaw described in Chapter Six. In this sense, the jigsaw metaphor has an emotional dimension.

As discussed in Chapter Three, information exchanged between professionals is a product of (ever more coercive) design rather than something that occurs naturally. The way in which policy directives attempt to 'standardise' the organisation of information, and determine what information is, thus becomes part of the problem; rational-bureaucratic determinism renders emotions as inadequate grounds on which to act. As such, organisational constraints restrict the passing on of feelings, or make emotion information difficult to express in organisational terms. We are forced to ask what can be 'cemented' on to professional feelings in order to make something 'legitimate' that can be passed to someone else to act on. The EWO's feelings, described in the earlier interview extract, were translated into something more tangible – a 'dirty house'. Importantly, this highlights a fundamental issue in the work of 'translation', in that it 'fills in' the gap between uncertain feelings, the sense that is made of emotion information, what is 'actually' observed, and the action taken. What we learn by the process of translation is that it blurs what is actually to be dealt with, and transforms it into something that is organisationally relevant, as well as something that may be very different from how it started out (for example, as a feeling). A process of further translation then has to take place by the information recipient, and thus the origins of the issue and what it means may become even further removed or 'diluted' from the original. This creates confusion. An example of this is when social workers go out and do not see what they expect to see from the information presented and from concerns suggested on the original referral form.

This chapter has shown that emotion information is very powerful in the way that it not only drives action but also shapes it in ways that consciously re-depict the scene/object for practical (emotion-related) purposes. This is particularly apparent in the accounts of two family support workers, which describe how what is observed and what is recorded become two different things. These extracts highlight how cases are 'talked down' for the sake of preserving working relationships with families, and also for fear of cross-examination in court. Emotion information may therefore play a role in why referrers 'talk up' the information they share at the referral stage, and why professionals do not see what they expect to see when they go out and do an assessment. This may also explain why social workers often regard received information as 'incomplete' – it is based on speculation, as emotion information drives referrers to pass on their 'hunches' rather than holding on to them for longer than necessary ('respectful uncertainty') or acting themselves. If not adequately addressed, a consequence of professionals' emotion information behaviour may be high rates of referral and re-referral of cases that may not require social work intervention at that point. This is particularly the case when emotion information is triggered by 'anticipatories' (of what might happen to a child in the future). As shown in the final three interview extracts in this chapter, these anxieties are managed by passing on what professionals 'think may happen' to children's services in the form of a referral.

A further area explored in this chapter is accurate recording practices. Returning to the family support workers' narratives, both extracts suggest that what comes with greater 'experience' and 'confidence' is a reduction of the influence of emotion information on recording practices. I also drew on professional 'experience' in my field notes from observations of initial assessment teams. My reflections at the time were that greater 'experience' appeared to contribute to social workers being more 'transparent' about emotions, and that emotions actively informed decisions relating to their contacts and whether cases should be opened up as referrals. However, on reflection some years later, I find it difficult to differentiate whether feelings are indeed a 'unique' reaction to what professionals are presented with on a case-by-case basis or 'incidental' in that these feelings derive, and are carried over, from similar situations they have encountered in the past. Commentators have suggested that people are usually unaware that emotions induced in one situation influence judgements made in another (Johnson and Tversky, 1983; Wilson and Brekke, 1996). Thus, in the everyday work of child protection, the 'advisory' role of emotion information in decision making, as a basis for guiding action, becomes potentially problematic; professionals are continually faced with new and unique circumstances, which, although often familiar, are never entirely the same. I would therefore suggest that there is a need for professional reflexivity on the emotionality of safeguarding work, examining how, and to what extent emotions guide and shape information-sharing activity, and further exploring how feelings can be communicated with other professionals to help understand what is being passed on. Emotions are embedded within social structures that make them meaningful. More importantly, 'Feelings are not substances to be discovered in our blood but social practices organised by stories that we both enact and tell' (Rosaldo, cited in Boellstorff and Lindquist, 2004, p 437). It is thus time to move away from the pervasiveness of 'objective' professional 'assessment' to a full appreciation of emotion information, and how this drives information-related behaviours that recast what issues professionals such as social workers actually deal with, for example, on a referral form.

Managers' questions for reflection

1. What forum can be created to explore how feelings can be communicated in helping to understand what is being passed on?
2. In response to this question, how might referral and assessment teams be reconfigured to respond to professional hunches or uncertain feelings to ensure that referrals received actually relate to concerns about a child, and that the 'right' children are receiving a service?

Professional questions for reflection

1. In relation to your work with children, when do you feel most anxious? What are the causes of your anxiety, and how do you manage it in your day-to-day work?
2. Are there any opportunities where you are able to discuss your feelings with other professionals? Is there anything that stops you being open about your feelings, or expressing a 'hunch' that something is 'not right' about a child?
3. How important are relationships in facilitating discussion about feelings and about what information is or is not shared?
4. Do you think about how something makes you feel when you are recording information? What do you do about those feelings, and how do you articulate them? Do your feelings alter the way in which you work with information?

NINE

Conclusion

What is to be done ought not to be determined from above by reformers, be they prophetic or legislative, but by a long work of comings and goings, of exchanges, reflections, trials, different analyses. (Foucault, 1981, p 13)

Many of the policies and initiatives, as well as much of the literature relating to child welfare, have been driven by failures to share, interpret or organise information. Current policies champion initiatives such as multi-agency safeguarding hubs (MASHs) and other forms of multi-agency working with children and families. Such initiatives are supported by the Centre of Excellence for Information Sharing and are heralded as a means to prevent children from slipping through the safeguarding 'net' by improving information sharing between professionals in order to gain a 'full' picture of children's and families' lives. However, as the chapters in the book have shown, and as many have observed over more than four decades, getting information sharing *right* is difficult. Successive public inquiries remind us that when things go wrong it is often because professionals have failed to share crucial information. This needs to be seen, however, in the context of short-staffed local authority referral and assessment teams, who struggle to ensure appropriate information responses when they are swamped by referrals and subsequent increases in the thresholds criteria for managing demand and resources). Even when information is shared, practice reviews report that miscommunication can occur – things get lost in translation, misread or misunderstood in information exchange processes.

Organisations such as children's services have complex systems for processing the information they receive from other professionals and the public. Social workers are the 'authorised' professionals for receiving, rationalising and dealing with referred information, carrying out assessments, and deciding what interventions should follow. Nevertheless, and in what could be regarded as a rather simplistic solution, central government responses to failures in information sharing continue to focus on modifications (improvements) to infrastructures aimed at supporting information recording and exchange, such as more sophisticated information technologies, more detailed guidance or legislation designed to remove apparent barriers hindering effective information-sharing practices. There are issues, however, with this type of response. For example, children's lives are increasingly regarded in terms of fragments of information, or 'bits and bytes' to be pieced together. Furthermore, there are concerns that technologies themselves may hinder information flow between professionals, and that everyday child welfare practices do not lend themselves to such modern information and communication technologies (Peckover et al, 2008, p 391; Broadhurst et al, 2010). A raft of organisational and bureaucratic changes continue to be made, yet time and time again, serious case reviews and public inquiry reports continue to highlight the same information failures. As such, 'information sharing' across organisational boundaries continues to attract 'formal' questioning, and is the focus of research priorities (DfE, 2014). An example of such research is the Child Protection Information Sharing project (CP-IS), which seeks to improve information flows, particularly between NHS hospitals and children's social care, through the development of a database housing information on children. The project covers areas such as child protection plans; looked-after children; and pregnant mothers whose unborn babies are subject to a pre-birth child protection plan (Health and Social Care Information Centre, 2014). 'Improvement' initiatives that aim to strengthen information sharing in child protection, alongside developments such as the establishment of a Centre of Excellence for Information Sharing, indicate that 'information sharing' is an area of practice likely to remain current on the child welfare agenda.

This book has sought to take up the challenge of understanding information practices on the ground, with a view to rendering visible some of the less well-documented activities, nuances and micro-patterns of information behaviour. In this context, the objective has been to stimulate new ways of thinking about information sharing and its inherent complexity by introducing such matters as professional needs and information-related behaviours, 'emotion information', 'information relationships' and the practical work of building 'full pictures' of children's lives akin to assembling pieces of a jigsaw. My initial aim was to cast more light on 'information-sharing' practices, including the referral process, which originally stemmed from work undertaken to help a local authority address concerns about high referral rates. However, I would argue that the observations made and the questions that have been raised can speak to multi-agency professionals tasked with safeguarding children, as well as policymakers, both nationally and internationally. In taking a social constructionist position, I have problematised the notion of 'information' that is otherwise frequently taken for granted in policy, legislation and practice discourse. Empirical findings in this book have challenged objectivist assumptions about the stability of meaning within child welfare information practices that assume that each professional using her/his particular language can elicit information that is finite and stable.

A number of authors have already drawn attention to one of the topics addressed in this book that lies at the heart of information exchange – and that is 'sense making' (White, 2009). This is important because it highlights that factors other than non-compliance or inadequate systems are at work to undermine effective information practices. Thus, the stock vocabulary of 'information sharing', and the prescriptions and procedures contained in official documents such as *Working together* (DHSS and Welsh Office, 1988; Home Office et al, 1991; DH et al, 1999; HM Government, 2006a, 2010a, 2013; 2015a) and other information-sharing guidance (HM Government, 2015b), gloss over an 'indeterminate zone of practice' (Klein, 2004, p 4). They do not reflect the situated contexts in which information sharing takes place, that is, how information is interpreted, translated and made sense of in different contexts. Therefore, and as this book demonstrates, the vocabulary of 'information sharing' needs broadening to extend current understandings of 'information sharing' in terms of system and purpose as contained in official information-sharing guidance (HM Government, 2015b). A shift in focus is required from how multi-agency professionals can get better at sharing information towards what prompts them to do it at all. As discussed in Chapter Four, this change in focus is driven by the blurring of professional boundaries around processes that best address the needs of children and families. In Chapter Four, we are urged to ask important questions such as what contexts can be created to share professional needs to understand what issues (i.e. uncertainty, fear, anxiety etc.) that receivers (for example social workers in referral and assessment teams) are actually dealing with In Chapter Four, we are urged to ask important questions such as how to help professionals understand the issues (such as uncertainty, fear, anxiety and so on) that receivers (for example, social workers in referral and assessment teams) have to deal with. Information grounds introduced in this chapter may be significant in terms of how professional needs are best shared, that is what form of information exchange would better deal with this issue. Different information loci (case conferences, core group or strategy meetings, conversations in cars, home visits, supervision sessions and so on) were seen to encourage different types of information sharing.

Inevitably, this book has questioned the idea that information sharing is merely a matter of diligent professionals passing on of 'knowledge' in order to build a 'full' picture of the lives of children and families; 'information sharing' is a more complex activity than suggested by standardised procedures and mantras that urge professionals simply to get better at doing it. Such an approach is flawed, as it leads only to a false sense that procedural changes will effect the necessary changes in practice. While I do not claim to have many of the answers to solve current issues in 'information sharing', I consider that initiatives to improve information practices continue to be overly mechanistic and based on assumptions of linear 'flows', and over many years have not yielded the desired improvements in performance in this area of professional work. This line of thinking sits with traditional information theory, which considers that information can simply be transacted as long as it is clear and not clouded by 'noise' (White et al, 2015, p 49). More recent theory, however, acknowledges that information has to be translated within and across organisational boundaries, and in doing so, undergoes a number of transformations (White et al, 2015, p 49). Now that the complexity of information practices in multi-agency work with children and families has been brought to the fore, it is time for policymakers to enter into meaningful dialogue with frontline professionals as to how information works in practice, so that new ways of working can emerge.

The multi-professional narratives in this book are clear. Professionals tasked with safeguarding children are committed to protecting and promoting the welfare of the children and families they work with. They are further committed to working together and sharing information in order to do so. What is also clear is that there are a number of factors that get in the way of doing this. While professionals comply with procedure, it is difficult to legislate for all of the complexities that arise in information practices. Professionals need to question what information is and is not contested, and why, as individual practitioners, within teams, during supervision sessions, and so forth (Taylor and White, 2000). Closer attention needs to be paid to the human factors that influence how information gets shared; and it is important for professionals to question their understanding and gain a reflexive awareness of processes of sense making, translation and transaction in complex interactions. As human information processors, professionals are subject to 'confirmation bias' (and a whole range of other information processing shortcuts and biases), which can lead to a 'misreading' of cases, situations and meaning. Moreover, professionals are often required to make decisions on the basis of speculative or ambiguous information, against a background of time constraints and other resource demands. Such factors continue to be demonstrated in Serious Case Reviews, however the inherent complexities of professional sense-making including the difficulties of establishing what is relevant information. Serious case reviews continue to highlight failures in information-sharing practices, but the inherent complexities of professional sense making include the difficulties of establishing what is relevant information. This is further complicated by additional factors discussed in this book, such as the implications of early categorisation, and anchoring onto a first hypothesis, discussed in Chapter Two. Highlighting these issues, White and colleagues (2015, p 14; emphasis in original) observe in relation to death of 17-month-old Peter Connelly ('Baby P') in 2007:

> Peter was observed to be injured very frequently, with a variety of bruises and bumps which became increasingly serious over time. However, Tracey Connelly, Peter's mother, alleged that he would frequently injure himself and have behavioural disturbances such as head banging, which were also observed by the social worker. A strong (but *wrong*) hypothesis thus took hold that Peter had a behavioural disorder. In his last few months of his life, Peter's weight was falling dramatically. His father has also raised concerns, and told agencies that Tracey Connelly had a new boyfriend. Many agencies were involved with Peter, but the different professionals seemed to be failing to notice or respond to the deterioration in Peter's health and development, and to act appropriately in relation to his injuries. Tracey Connelly had been apparently co-operative with services, frequently presenting Peter at the doctor's surgery, for example to seek help with what she said was his difficult behaviour.

What White and colleagues make clear is that professionals involved in the case had committed to the hypothesis of Peter being 'behaviourally disturbed'. However, in doing so, they had also formed a full picture. The case construction (picture/frame) was complete and new 'pieces' of information simply slotted into that frame so that a particular reading of the case endured. This 'reading' of the case by professionals was secured through Tracey Connelly's cooperation with professionals she came into contact with, and further by her requests for help in finding ways of dealing with Peter's alleged 'challenging' behaviour. On this basis, it is easy to understand how the case continued to be misread.

While professionals operate on the basis of 'background expectancies' and within frameworks that help identify cases of child 'abuse', it is always the *sense* that is made of an event, action or symptom that prevails rather than the material property of the 'thing itself'. However, as Chapter Two highlights, meaning attribution is bound up with connection; that is, meaning derives from the connections that are drawn between pieces, rather than the pieces of the jigsaw themselves. The work of sense making is also situated, and context cannot simply be reduced to the role of the professional; it also involves the immediate context of just prior interpretations to which subsequent interpretations are added. Thus, meaning making is always in process: meaning derives from *connections* that are made between 'pieces' or 'snippets' of information, rather than emerging *directly* from individual 'pieces'. Meaning making thus has a complex temporal quality – that is, it is achieved at particular points in time, but can also change in time and place. A 'piece' can be depicted in a myriad of ways; organisational relevance determines what meaning is attributed to a 'piece' in order to establish a 'full' picture. There is thus a need for training in skills of analysis that recognise the socially constructed nature of information, with close scrutiny of sense making in professional case formulation work. Drawing on key themes from this book, training needs to centre on how professionals form connections and relationships with information, as well as considering professional positioning to information and reaching a shared understanding about what information different professionals can reasonably obtain and share with other agencies.

Building a 'full' picture and assumed 'endpoints'

Pictures of child welfare concerns can only be built in the context, or within boundaries, of organisations. Chapter Six highlights how gathering a 'full' picture does not comprise gathering 'pieces' that are universally available to a multi-professional workforce, but rather how the process of building pictures is situated; each professional assembles available pieces within different contexts, which have particular relevant indicators of child concern within that particular context. This observation chimes with the assumed relativism of policy and legislative guidance. However, what it is important is that a 'picture' or 'pictures' can shift through the actions of other agencies, and these actions may have less to do with organisational descriptors of child concern and more to do with agencies' immediate organisational priorities or relevance, which can prompt a pictures 'endpoint'. Thus, endpoints are not achieved by obtaining a full (universal) picture of a child; rather, they are illusive, often partial, and may involve passing work on, deflecting work elsewhere (for example if social workers think it is 'not for us to deal with'), or closing a case. Such endpoints are not likely to be explicitly shared with, or known by, other agencies. Professionals need to consider dismantling their own and others' 'full pictures' – the jigsaw is never complete, rather it is always changing. A child's or family's life is more akin to the changing pictures of a kaleidoscope (that is, comprising a number of constructions) as opposed to a static picture fostered in practice by the use of the jigsaw metaphor. It is also important to note that while there are different endpoints for different agencies, these endpoints may solidify into a multi-agency picture, reflecting the predisposition of groups towards agreement.

Filtering work can operate on the basis of organisational relevance; material deemed organisationally 'irrelevant' (such as social workers as receivers of a referral) becomes invisible in this process. This process of filtering explains why agencies lose information, or miss or fail to make connections, as in the Peter Connelly case. A practical question then arises as to how we identify the invisible. At best, we can achieve closer reflexive awareness of filtering processes in information transactions between professionals, and increase awareness of why/how information gets left out of the pictures that are created and passed on to other agencies. Professionals' accounts in Chapter Six show how it is possible for a number of professionals to be involved in a case but apparently miss signs of child maltreatment, as each professional appears to be trying to reach their own organisationally relevant 'endpoint'. Each endpoint is therefore not about the needs of children and families per se, but rather an organisational imperative that is unlikely to be understood by those outside of an agency's organisational boundary. However, recent research suggests that multi-agency safeguarding hubs

(MASHs) promote better understanding between professions (Home Office, 2014), so organisational imperatives are likely to be more transparent where such arrangements exist.

Embodied relationships and relationships with information

It is well established that relationships between people are important for working together and sharing information. Research indicates that the establishment of MASHs and the co-location of professionals has improved the quality of information relationships at the national level (Home Office, 2014), and there is further anecdotal evidence to suggest that MASHs have enabled the timely sharing of vital information. While these findings may reflect practice realities for some, this will certainly not be the case for all, as other factors can get in the way of good information sharing. For example, while trust and reciprocity were shown in Chapter Seven to be significant for fostering effective information-sharing relationships, the way these factors operate in practice has been shown to be far from straightforward. Reciprocity between agencies must be seen to be reliable, not sporadic, regardless of how valuable the available information may/could be. Although information relationships are to some extent mandatory, there is still room for individual variation in performance, as Chapter Seven shows. Another significant factor is the moral quality of embodied relationships, which can determine whether the action of sharing information is 'superficial' or more 'meaningful'. Given this observation, the question then arises as to how voluntary networks can be strengthened, and further, how can these networks be maintained, particularly in the context of worker turnover and frequent structural and organisational change. Morrison (1996, p 130) comments on the complexity of 'working together' and suggests that it requires contact between varying emotional realities, different systems of meaning, and varying types of bias. MASH arrangements that establish effective working cultures and processes may help break down these differences (Home Office, 2014, p 8), but this is by no means a given.

Chapter Seven brought to the fore professionals' relationships with information. Information relationships are different from embodied relationships between people, although the two types can exist in parallel, with the latter often affecting relationships with information. Professionals are positioned differently in regard to information and have different information requirements defined by their organisational 'hats'. This evokes concerns that were central to the development of the Common Assessment Framework and similar guidance documents (DfES, 2004a). Organisational boundaries construct what information is relevant, or what is valued in terms of information requirements. Fundamentally, this influences the relationship individuals have with information, the connections that people make, or fail to make, and the work they do with information they 'gather' or receive. Professional relationships to information are not static but are subject to change depending on the task at hand (for example, Ofsted inspections, assessments and so forth). This is as an indicator for establishing how matters get missed, deprioritised or remain unconnected (in other words, the relationship with information is not established), or get picked up and 'pieced together' somewhat arbitrarily. Information relationships may explain how it is that calls for better information sharing are not wholly resolved by improving 'working together' per se – including the implementation of MASH models – if such matters are not addressed.

Emotion information

While emotions in child protection work have been discussed at length elsewhere, this book charts new ground in its exploration of how emotion information influences other information-related behaviours. Importantly, emotion information poses some problems for professionals given the current organisation of child welfare services. Feelings about children are not necessarily substantiated by clear 'evidence' of child protection issues (that is, they are not 'facts' that can be clearly communicated). Emotion information is not 'hearable' in the same way as, for example, medical evidence. In their interviews, professionals described feelings as difficult to articulate for referral purposes and regarded them as insufficient grounds on which to act. This may cause frontline workers to attempt to identify something more concrete or tangible, but which may not match the level of emotion information or feeling experienced. Here we encounter another type of translation work. Feelings have to be 'translated' into something more substantive in order to make a referral. Emotions are at the boundary of referral making, but are difficult to express in organisational terms. Information is much more than an 'object' to be passed on – 'emotion information' becomes translated into 'non-emotion information' in order to achieve a response to, or satisfaction of, emotion needs. Professionals need to consider, and carefully reflect upon, that they may be seeking tangible examples from family life which express an anxiety or other emotion they are feeling.

Chapter Eight explores professional 'needs' that can drive information-related behaviours, such as making a referral to children's services. This raises a practical question about service development in terms of how emotions are communicated in child protection work. What spaces can be created, or information grounds identified, for their articulation? Where professionals' emotion needs remain unmet, there may be an increase in referral rates as a way of managing anxiety. In terms of budgets, the space/time for (in)formal conversation between referrers and workers within and between agencies can be squeezed. Furthermore, information and communication technologies may replace other forms of embodied communication, leaving even less room for face-to-face dialogue. Professionals in referral *transactions* need to be able to engage in open and honest dialogue, to deal with suspicions, hunches and so forth; the quality of relationships (and time and space) determines whether this will or can take place.

Emotion information can trigger 'anticipatories' or 'imaginaries' – visions/sketches of what might happen to a child based on the worst-case scenarios of a child's death. We can see in Chapter Eight that sense making is based not just on the here and now, but also the imagined or predicted, which ultimately places a burden at the front door of children's services. Sense making enters the world of (professional) 'fiction' in the quest to look to the future for a child and their family. Emotion is a powerful driver of the imagination. Emotion information is also central to how incoming data is used, such that it may have more to do with workflow anxieties than emotion information arising from face-to-face direct interaction with children. In some cases, when professionals formally pass on information, what they are in fact doing is managing their feelings or ambivalent *concerns*. It is therefore important to consider what happens when a case is passed to another service via a referral. It may be that a referrer revises her/his opinion in light of the local authority's response (the situation is being dealt with, the situation is or is not a concern because the local authority has assessed it), when it would be better for the local authority to reinforce the message that initial assessment queries are not entirely conclusive. In this sense, and drawing on the key themes of this book more broadly, conversations need to take place between professionals to generate clear understandings of professionals' (mis)interpretative practices.

Concluding remarks

Messages from public inquiry reports into the deaths of children, and related policy dictates, do not convey the complexities of information practices in the day-to-day work of safeguarding children. Rather, they gloss over the complexities of 'information sharing' in *practice,* and how this is achieved in the context of organisational and procedural requirements, professional cultures and individual interpretation and understanding. It is only by considering the human factors highlighted in this book that new questions, conversations and possibilities can emerge – having the potential to recast information practices in the direction of policymaking rather than continuing as unsuccessful pursuits. This book has shown that understanding what information is and what it means requires a more significant complex set of ideas than is currently offered in policy and practice dictates. Thus, it is hoped that this book will provide the impetus for policymakers and managers to design services with communication in mind, using Foucault's suggestion at the opening of this chapter to guide how optimum service design in child protection may be achieved.

APPENDIX 1

**Children & Young
People's Department**

Children in Need Model

Level 4

Children at risk of significant harm / or has suffered abuse and for whom there is continued risk.
Child in household where parents/carers have mental health, substance dependency or domestic abuse issues which put child at risk of significant harm. | Persons identified as posing a risk to child identified as living in the house. | The child's life is endangered. | There is evidence of serious or significant injury or illness. | The possibility of non-accidental injury. | Evidence of gross neglect. | Children who are persistently missing from home and who put themselves at significant risk. | Actually homeless and no housing agency able or willing to assist. | Unsanitary or dangerous home conditions. | Sexual exploitation and/or abuse. | Serious injury/ harm/abuse to self or other. | Seriously challenging behaviour. | A child abandoned. | Life threatening drug abuse. | Trafficked child. | Risk of long-term psychological damage/deprivation. | Significant impairment of physical/emotional development. | Damaging history of separations. | Children at risk of forced marriage. | Children who abuse other children.

Level 3
Children whose vulnerability is such that they are unlikely to reach or maintain a satisfactory level of health or development.

Level 3b
Children with disabilities. | Children with high level needs whose parents, for whatever reason, are unable to meet those needs. | Children from families where there has been one serious or several significant instances of domestic violence. | Children where a CAF Action Plan has had no significant impact. | Children who have been subject to a CP Plan, or who have been previously looked after where there are new/further concerns. | Children with high level/unassessed needs whose parents have a history of non-engagement with services, or fail to recognise concerns of professionals. | Pregnant women where the safety of the unborn child might be compromised. | Children in families experiencing a crisis that is likely to result in a breakdown of care arrangements. | Persistent and serious offending. | Unaccompanied asylum seekers.

Level 3a
Children who are persistently going missing from home. | Children with a significant emotional and/or behavioural disorder. | Young carers. | Children with chronic absence from school. | Children in families without permanent accommodation. | Children with chronic ill health/terminal illness. | Children involved in substance misuse. | Child in households where parenting is compromised as a consequence of parental discord, mental health, substance misuse or domestic abuse, although child's needs are not at a high level. | Children and young people involved in acrimonious contact/residence disputes. | Children who are experiencing adverse effects from bullying.

Level 2
Disadvantaged children who would benefit from extra help to make the best life chances. Services operating at a preventative level.
Parents unable to secure some aspects of health or development; poor health; poor school attendance. | Inappropriate age related behaviour which is difficult to handle. | Inhibited/restricted development opportunities in own home and community. | Demands of caring for another person undermining aspects of health and development. | Poor standard of physical care or health causing concern; unhealthy diet; unsatisfactory accommodation. | Insufficient stimulation to achieve full potential; no opportunities to play with other children; experiencing difficulties in relationship with peers. | Scape-goating or victimisation causing emotional harm including continual/regular periods of stress, conflict, tension causing instability and insecurity in relationships; absence of appropriate stimulation. | Relationships strained; normal health and development constrained by environmental circumstances and/or limited play opportunities.

Level 1
All children within the borough and who are routinely in receipt of community services. Assumes backdrop of universal Education and Health services.

Multi-agency interview schedule used in phase two of data collection

1. How does your workload come in to you?
2. How do concerns or issues about a child/family arise?
3. What do you understand to be your main role?
4. What do you understand as your subsidiary/secondary role?
5. Could you give me an account of a typical case from beginning to end and tell me why this is case is regarded as 'typical'?
6. Could you give me an account of a untypical case from the beginning to end and tell me why this case is not regarded as typical?
7. Do you think that your case examples could be dealt with by an alternative agency or in a different way (e.g. using informal networks more)?
8. What are your agency's strengths in working with vulnerable families?
9. What are your agency's limitations in working with vulnerable families?
10. What information do you need to deal with or identify any concerns and issues regarding children and families (i.e. growth charts, education records, housing records and so on)?
11. Is that (information) the same for others you work with?
12. Do you think practices vary with regards to what information is needed to deal with or identify concerns and issues with children and families? If yes, how do practices vary?

13. What kinds of records do you keep? When and how are these records used?

14. What are your policies and procedures regarding record keeping generally (i.e. filing system, which bits of cases are kept/filed and which information is disregarded)? How is the IT system/ telephone used/depended on?

15. Do you accept information given to you? When would you research the information further and how would you do this?

16. What information would you consider is hard to get hold of?

17. What information would you consider is easy to get hold of?

18. What concerns or issues would lead you to refer to social services? Could you give two or three examples of these concerns (and all the details) and tell me how you were first alerted to these concerns and also what you did?

19. What information do you feel you need to confidently refer to social services (i.e. a comment, a report from another professional, discussion with a supervisor to reach agreement whether to make a referral)l?

20. What are your expectations of social services once you have made a referral to them?

21. What is your understanding of social services' referral process and threshold criteria?

22. When would you seek more or further information from a child in relation to information you've been given that causes concern?

23. When would you seek more or further information from a carer in relation to information you've been given that causes concern?

24. Are there any concerns or issues that you would refer to agencies other than social services? (Think of some examples and ask what information the professional being interviewed needs to do that – would they discuss this with a supervisor, does certain information make concerns straightforward?)

25. Do you think the referral process is working?

References

Alfaro, J. (1988) What can we learn from child abuse fatalities? A synthesis of nine studies, in D.J. Besharov (ed), *Protecting children from abuse and neglect: Policy and practice*, Springfield, IL: Charles C. Thomas.

Anderson, D.G. (2000) Coping strategies and burnout among veteran child protection workers, *Child Abuse and Neglect*, 24(6): 839–48.

Austin, J.L. (1962) *How to do things with words*, Oxford: Clarendon.

Australian Commission on Safety and Quality in Health Care (2008) *Clinical handover: A literature review*, Sydney: Australian Commission on Safety and Quality in Health Care.

Axford, N. (2008) Is social exclusion a useful concept in children's services?, *British Journal of Social Work*, advanced access, doi: 10.1093/bjsw/bcn121

Bauman, Z. (1989) *Freedom*, Milton Keynes: Open University Press.

Beck, U. (1992) *Risk society: Towards a new modernity*, London: Sage.

Benson, D. and Hughes, J.A. (1983) *The perspective of ethnomethodology*, London: Addison-Wesley Longman.

Berger, P.L. and Luckmann, T. (1966) *The social construction of reality: A treatise in the sociology of knowledge*, USA: Doubleday.

Bichard, M. (2004) *The Bichard inquiry report*, London: TSO.

Birmingham LSCB (Local Safeguarding Children Board) (2010) *Serious case review under chapter VIII 'Working together to safeguard children' in respect of the death of a child, Case Number 14*, available at: http://northumberlandlscb.proceduresonline.com/pdfs/kyhra_ishaq_scr.pdf (last accessed 8/12/15).

Blair, D. (2006) *Wittgenstein, language and information: 'Back to the rough ground!'* Berlin: Springer.

Boden, D. (1994) *The business of talk: Organizations in action*, Cambridge: Polity.

Boellstorff, T. and Lindquist, J. (2004) Bodies of emotion: rethinking culture and emotion through Southeast Asia, *Ethnos*, 69(4): 437–444.

Bradford Safeguarding Children Board (2013) *A serious case review: Hamzah Khan: The overview report*, available at: http://www.bradford-scb.org.uk/scr/hamzah_khan_scr/Serious%20Case%20Reveiw%20Overview%20Report%20November%202013.pdf

Brandon, M., Owers, M. and Black, J (1999) *Learning how to make children safer: An analysis for the Welsh Office of serious child abuse cases in Wales*, Norwich: University of East Anglia/Welsh Office.

Brandon, M., Belderson, P., Warren, C., Howe, D., Gardner, R., Dodsworth, J. and Black, J. (2008) *Analysing child deaths and serious injury through abuse and neglect: What can we learn?*, DCSF.

Brashers, D.E. (2001) Communication and uncertainty management, *Journal of Communication*, 51: 477–97

Braun, V. and Clarke, V. (2006) Using thematic analysis in psychology, *Qualitative Research in Psychology*, 3: 77–101.

Broadhurst, K. (2007) Parental help-seeking and the moral order. Notes for policy makers and parenting practitioners on 'the First Port of Call' and 'No One to Turn to', *Sociological Research Online*, 12(6): 4, available at: http://www.socresonline.org.uk/12/6/4/4.pdf (last accessed 20/08/15).

Broadhurst, K., Grover, C. and Jamieson, J. (eds) (2009) *Critical perspectives on safeguarding children*, Chichester: Wiley–Blackwell.

Broadhurst, K., Wastell, D., White, S., Hall, C., Peckover, S., Thompson, K., Pithouse, A. and Dolores, D. (2010) Performing initial assessment: identifying the latent conditions for error in local authority children's services, *British Journal of Social Work*, 40(2): 352–70.

Brown, J.S. and Duguid, P. (2000) *The social life of information*, Boston, MA: Harvard Business School Press.

Butler, I. and Drakeford, M. (2005) *Scandal, social policy and social welfare*, Bristol: Policy Press.

Byles, J.A. (1985) Problems in inter-agency collaboration: lessons from a project that failed, *Child Abuse and Neglect*, 9: 549–54.

Byrne, D. (1998) *Complexity and the social sciences*, London: Routledge.

Cabinet Office Social Exclusion Task Force (2008) *Think family: Improving the life chances of families at risk*, London: Social Exclusion Unit.

Campbell, M. and Gregor, F. (2002) *Mapping social relations: A primer in doing institutional ethnography*, Aurora, ON: Garamond.

Case, D. (2004) *Looking for information: A survey of research on information seeking, needs, and behavior*, London: Academic Press.

Chang, V.Y., Arora, V.M., Lev-Ari, S., D'Arcy, M. and Keysar, B. (2010) Interns overestimate the effectiveness of their hand-off communication, *Pediatrics*, 125(3): 491–96.

Chatman, E.A. (2000) Framing social life in theory and research, *New review of information behaviour research: Studies of information seeking in context*, 1: 3-17.

Clarke, J., Gewirtz, S. and McLaughlin, E. (eds) (2000) *New managerialism new welfare?* London: Sage.

Cleaver, H., Unel, I. and Aldgate, J. (1999) *Children's needs – parenting capacity: The impact of parental mental illness, problem alcohol and drug use, and domestic violence on children's development*, London: TSO.

Cleaver, H., Cleaver, D., Cleaver, D. and Woodhead, V. (2004) *Information sharing and assessment: The progress of 'non-trailblazer' Local Authorities*, Research Report, 566, London: DfES.

Cohen, S. (2001) *States of denial: Knowing about atrocities and suffering*, London: John Wiley.

Colwell Report (1974) *Report of the Committee of Inquiry into the care and supervision provided in relation to Maria Colwell*, London: HMSO.

Cooper, A. (2005) Surface and depth in the Victoria Climbié Inquiry Report, *Child and Family Social Work*, 10: 1–9.

Corby, B. (2006) *Child abuse: Towards a knowledge base*, Maidenhead: Open University Press.

Coventry LSCB (Local Safeguarding Children Board) (2013) *Serious Case Review (overview report): Daniel Pelka*, available at: http://moderngov.coventry.gov.uk/documents/s13038/ Daniel%20Pelka%20Serious%20Case%20Review%20SCR. pdf (last accessed 21/02/2015).

Creedon, S. (2005) Health care workers' hand decontamination practices: compliance with recommended guidelines, *Journal of Advanced Nursing*, 51(3): 208–16.

CWDC (Children's Workforce Development Council) (2008) *Progress towards integrated working: 2007/2008 evaluation*, available at: http://dera.ioe.ac.uk/1844/1/IW67-0109_Progress_Towards_Integrated_Working_Full_Report.pdf (last accessed 24/02/16).

Dale, P., Green R. and Fellows, R. (2002) *What really happened? Child protection case management of infants with serious injuries and discrepant parental explanations*, London: NSPCC.

Damasio, A.R. (1994) *Descartes' error: Emotion, reason, and the human brain*, New York, NY: Putnam.

Davies, E. and McKenzie, P.J. (2004) Preparing for opening night: temporal boundary objects in textually-mediated professional practice, *Information Research*, 10(1): paper 211, available at: http://www.informationr.net/ir/10-1/paper211.html

DCSF (Department for Children, Schools and Families) (2007) *The children's plan: Building brighter futures*, London: TSO.

DCFS (2009) *Safeguarding disabled children practice guidance*, London: DCFS, available at: https://www.gov.uk/government/uploads/system/uploads/attachment_data/file/190544/00374-2009DOM-EN.pdf

DCSF (2010) *Embedding information sharing toolkit*, London: DCSF.

DCSF and CLG (Communities and Local Government) (2008) *Information sharing: A guide for practitioners and managers*, London: DCSF.

Derrida, J. (1981) *Dissemination. Translation, annotation, and introduction by Barbara Johnson*, London: Athlone Press.

Dervin, B. (1992) From the mind's eye of the user: the sense-making qualitative-quantitative methodology, in J.D. Glazier and R.R. Powell (eds) *Qualitative research in information management*, Englewood, CO: Libraries Unlimited Inc.

DfE (Department for Education) (2014) *Child protection, social work reform and intervention: Research priorities and questions*, London: HMSO.

DfES (Department for Education and Skills) (2003) *Every child matters – The Green Paper*, Cm 5860, London: DfES.

DfES (2004a) *Every child matters – Next steps*, London: DfES.

DfES (2004b) *Every child matters – Change for children*, London: DfES.

DfES (2004c) *Common assessment framework consultation document* (August 2004), London: DfES

DH (Department of Health) (1988) *Report of the inquiry into child abuse in Cleveland, 1987*, Cm 412, London: HMSO.

DH (1995) *Child protection: Messages from research*, London: Stationery Office.

DH, Department of Education and Employment, and Home Office (2000) *Framework for the assessment of children in need and their families*, London: TSO.

DH, Home Office, and Department of Education and Employment (1999) *Working together to safeguard children: A guide to inter-agency working to safeguard and promote the welfare of children*, London: TSO.

DHSS (1970) *The battered baby*, CM 02/70.

DHSS (1972) *Battered babies*, LASSL 26/72.

DHSS (1974) *Non-accidental injury to children*, LASSL (74)(14).

DHSS and Welsh Office (1988) *Working together: A guide to arrangements for inter-agency co-operation for the protection of children from abuse*, London: HMSO.

Dingwall, R., Eekelaar, J. and Murray, T. (1983) *The protection of children: State intervention and family life*, Oxford: Basil Blackwell.

Dourish, P. (2004) *Where the action is: The foundations of embodied interaction*, Cambridge, MA: MIT.

Drew, P. and Heritage, J. (1992) Analyzing talk at work: an introduction, in P. Drew and J. Heritage (eds) *Talk at work: Interaction in institutional settings*, pp 3–65, Cambridge: Cambridge University Press.

Falkov, A. (1996) *Study of working together 'Part 8' reports. Fatal child abuse and parental psychiatric disorder: An analysis of 100 area child protection committee case reviews conducted under the terms of Part 8 of Working Together Under the Children Act 1989*, London: Department of Health.

Ferguson, H. (2007) Working with violence, the emotions and the psycho-social dynamics of child protection: reflections on the Victoria Climbié case, *Social Work Education*, 24(7): 781–95.

Fisher, K.E. and Naumer, C.M. (2006) Information grounds: theoretical basis and empirical findings on information flow in social settings, in A. Spink and C. Cole (eds) *New directions in human information behaviour.*, Dordrecht: Springer, 2006, 93–111.

Foray, D. and Lundvall B.-Å. (eds) (1996) *Employment and growth in the knowledge-based economy*, Paris: OECD.

Forsberg, H. and Vagli, A. (2006) The social construction of emotions in child protection case-talk, *Qualitative Social Work*, 5(1): 9–31.

Foucault, M. (1981) Questions of method, *Ideology and consciousness*, 8(3): 3–14.

Frothingham, T., Barnett, R., Hobbs, C. and Wynne, J. (1993) Child sexual abuse in Leeds before and after Cleveland, *Child Abuse Review*, 2: 23–34.

Garfinkel, H. (1967) *Studies in ethnomethodology*, Cambridge: Polity Press.

Gibb, J. (2001) Maintaining front-line workers in child protection: a case for refocusing supervision, *Child Abuse Review*, 10: 323–35.

Gilbert, M. (2005) *Churchill and America*, London: The Free Press.

Goffman, E. (1974) *Frame analysis: An essay on the organization of experience*, New York, NY: Harper and Row.

Goffman, E. (1981) *Forms of talk*, Philadelphia, PA: University of Pennsylvania Press.

Goldthorpe, L. (2004) Every child matters: a legal perspective, *Child Abuse Review*, 13: 115–36.

Gray, M., Midgley, J. and Webb, S. (eds) (2012) *The Sage handbook of social work*, London: Sage.

Gubrium, J.F., Buckholdt, D.R. and Lynott, R.J. (1989) The descriptive tyranny of forms, in J. Holstein and G. Miller (eds), *Perspectives on Social Problems, Vol 1*, pp 195–214.

Gutherson, P. and Pickard, E. (2007) *Information sharing, the common assessment framework and early support*, available at: http://www.ncb.org.uk/media/512177/information_sharing_the_common_assessment_framework_and_early_support.pdf Accessed 09/12/15.

Haig, K., Sutton, S. and Whittington, J. (2006) SBAR:A shared mental model for improving communication between clinicians, *Journal on Quality and Patient Safety*, 32(3): 167–75.

Hall, C. and Slembrouck, S. (2009) Professional categorization, risk management, and inter-agency communication in public inquiries into disastrous outcomes, *British Journal of Social Work*, 39(2): 280–98.

Hallett, C. and Birchall, E. (1992) *Co-ordination and child protection: A review of the literature*, London: Stationery Office.

Hallett, C. and Stevenson, O. (1980) *Child abuse: Aspects of interprofessional co-operation*, London: George Allan and Unwin.

Haringey LSCB (Local Safeguarding Children Board) (2008) *Serious case review 'Child A'. Executive summary, November*, London: Department for Education.

Haringey LSCB (2009) *Serious case review: Baby Peter. Executive summary*, available at: http://www.haringeylscb.org/sites/haringeylscb/files/executive_summary_peter_final.pdf Last accessed: 10/12/15.

Harrison, S. (1999) Clinical autonomy and health policy: past and futures, in M. Exworthy and S. Halford (eds), *Professionals and the new managerialism in the public sector*, Buckingham: Open University Press, pp 50–64.

Health and Social Care Information Centre (2014) Child Protection Information Sharing Project (CP-IS), available at: http://systems.hscic.gov.uk/cpis/needed/cpisfaqs.pdf Last accessed: 18/08/15.

Heritage, J. (1984) *Garfinkel and ethnomethodology*, Oxford: Basil Blackwell.

Hill, N. (2003) Civil liberty: under surveillance, *Young People Now*, 26 November.

HM Government (2002) *Investigating complex abuse*, London: HMSO.

HM Government (2003) *Female genital mutilation*, London: HMSO.

HM Government (2006a) *Working together to safeguard children: A guide to inter-agency working to safeguard and promote the welfare of children*, London: HMSO.

HM Government (2006b) *Information sharing: Guidance for professionals and managers*, London: DfES.

HM Government (2007a) *Safeguarding children from abuse linked to a belief in spirit possession*, London: DfES.

HM Government (2007b) *Safeguarding children who may have been trafficked*, London: DfE and Home Office.

HM Government (2008a) *Safeguarding children in whom illness is fabricated or induced. Supplementary guidance to Working Together to Safeguard Children*, London: DCSF.

HM Government (2008b) *Domestic violence, forced marriage and 'honour'-based violence. Government reply to the 6th report from the Home Affairs Committee Session 2007-08, HC 263*. Cm 7450, London: TSO.

HM Government (2008c) *The right to choose: Multi-agency statutory guidance for dealing with forced marriage*, London: Foreign and Commonwealth Office.

HM Government (2009a) *Safeguarding children and young people from sexual exploitation. Supplementary guidance to Working Together to Safeguard Children*, London: DCSF.

HM Government (2010a) *Working together to safeguard children: A guide to the inter-agency working to safeguard and promote the welfare of children*, London: DCSF.

HM Government (2010b) *Safeguarding children and young people who may be affected by gang activity*, London: DCFS and Home Office.

HM Government (2013) *Working together to safeguard children: A guide to inter-agency working to safeguard and promote the welfare of children*, London: HMSO.

HM Government (2015a) *Working together to safeguard children: A guide to inter-agency working to safeguard and promote the welfare of children*, London: HMSO.

HM Government (2015b) *Information sharing: Advice for practitioners providing safeguarding services to children, young people, parents and carers*, London: Department for Education.

HM Government (2015c) *What to do if you're worried a child is being abused: Advice for practitioners*, London: HMSO.

Hobbs C., Wynne, A. and Thomas, A. (1995a) Colposcopic genital findings in pre-pubertal girls assessed for sexual abuse, *Disease in Childhood*, (73): 465–71.

Hobbs, C., Wynne, J. and Gelletie, R. (1995b) Leeds inquiry into infant deaths: the importance of abuse and neglect in sudden infant death, *Child Abuse Review*, 4: 329–39.

Home Office (2014) *Multi-agency working and information sharing project*, London: Home Office.

Home Office, Department of Health, Department of Education and Science and the Welsh Office (1991) *Working together under the Children Act 1989: A guide to arrangements for inter-agency co-operation for the protection of children from abuse*, London: HMSO.

Hood, R. (2014) Complexity and integrated working in children's services, *British Journal of Social Work* (44): 27–43.

House of Commons Education and Skills Committee (2005) *Every child matters. Ninth report of session 2004-05, volume 1*, London: HMSO.

Howe, D. (1992) Child abuse and the bureaucratisation of social work, *The Sociological Review*, 40(3): 491–508.

Howe, D. (1996) Surface and depth in social work practice, in N. Parton (ed), *Social theory, social change and social work*, London: Routledge.

Hudson, B. (2002) Interprofessionality in health and social care: the Achilles' heel of partnership, *Journal of Interprofessional Care*, 16: 1: 7–17.

Hudson, B. (2005a) Information sharing and children's services reform in England: can legislation change practice? *Journal of Interprofessional Care*, 19(6): 537–637.

Hudson, B. (2005b) User outcomes and children's services reform: ambiguity and conflict in the policy implementation process, *Social Policy and Society*, 5: 227–36.

Iedema, R., Merrick, E.T., Rajbhandari, D., Gardo, A., Stirling, A. and Herkes, R. (2009) Viewing the taken-for-granted from under a different aspect: a video-based method in pursuit of patient safety, *International Journal of Multiple Research Approaches*, 3(3): 290–301.

Johnson, J.D. (1997) *Cancer-related information seeking*, Cresskill, NJ: Hampton Press.

Johnson, E.J. and Tversky, A. (1983) Affect, generalization, and the perception of risk, *Journal of Personality and Social Psychology*, 45: 20–31.

Jones, R. (2014) *The story of Baby P: Setting the record straight*, Bristol: Policy Press.

King, M. and Piper, C. (1995) *How the law thinks about children* (second edition), Aldershot: Arena.

Klein, J.T. (2004) Interdisciplinarity and complexity: an evolving relationship, *E:CO Special Double Issue*, 6(1–2): 2–10.

Krikelas, J. (1983) Information seeking behaviour: patterns and concepts, *Drexel Library Quarterly*, 19(2): 5–20.

Kuijvenhoven, T. and Kortleven, W.J. (2010) Inquiries into fatal child abuse in the Netherlands: a source of improvement? *British Journal of Social Work*, 40: 1152–73.

Lachman, P. and Bernard, C. (2006) Moving from blame to quality: how to respond to failures in child protective services, *Child Abuse and Neglect*, 30(9): 963–68.

Laming, W.H.L. (2003) *The Victoria Climbié inquiry: Report of an inquiry by Lord Laming* (Cmnd 5730), London: Stationery Office.

Laming, W.H.L. (2009) *The protection of children in England: A progress report*, London: Stationery Office.

Law, J. and Mol, A. (eds) (2002) *Complexities*, Durham: Duke University Press.

Lee, C. (2007) Boundary negotiating artifacts: unbinding the routine of boundary objects and embracing chaos in collaborative work, *Computer Supportive Cooperative Work*, 16, 307–39.

Leonard, M., Graham, S. and Bonacum, D. (2004) The human factor: the critical importance of effective teamwork and communication in providing safe care, *Quality and Safety in Health Care*, 13: 85–90.

Lewin, D. and Herron, H. (2007) Signs, symptoms and risk factors: health visitors perspectives of child neglect, *Child Abuse Review*, 16: 93–107.

Lingard, L., Espin, S., Rubin, B., Whyte, S., Colmenares, M., Baker, G.R., Doran, D., Grober, E., Orser, B., Bohnen, J. and Reznick, R. (2005) Getting teams to talk: development and pilot implementation of a checklist to promote interprofessional communication in the OR, *Quality and Safety in Health Care*, 14: 340–46.

Lipsky, M. (1980) *Street level bureaucracy: Dilemmas of the individual in public services*, New York, NY: Russell Sage Foundation.

London Borough of Brent (1985) *A child in trust. Report of the panel of inquiry investigating the circumstances surrounding the death of Jasmine Beckford*, London: The London Boroughs.

London Borough of Greenwich (1987) *A child in mind: Protection of children in a responsible society. Report of the commission of inquiry into the circumstances surrounding the death of Kimberley Carlile*, London: Greenwich Social Services Department.

Luhmann, N. (1995) *Social systems*. Palo Alto, CA: Stanford University Press.

Lynch, M. and Bogen, D. (1996) *The spectacle of history: Speech, text and memory at the Iran-Contra hearings*, Durham, NC: Duke University Press.

Lyon, D. (1988) *The information society: Issues and illusions*, Cambridge: Polity Press.

Lyon, D. (2001) *Surveillance society: Monitoring everyday life*, Buckingham: Open University Press.

Martin, W.J. (1995) *The global information society*, Aldershot: Aslib/Gower.

Masson, J. (2006) The Climbié inquiry – context and critique, *Journal of Law and Society*, 33(2): 221–43.

May-Chahal, C. and Broadhurst, K. (2006) Integrating objects of intervention and organisational relevance: the case of safeguarding children missing from education systems, *Child Abuse Review*, 15: 440–55.

McGloin, P. and Turnbull, A. (1986) *Parental participation in child abuse review conferences*, London: London Borough of Greenwich.

McKenzie, P. (2006) Mapping textually mediated information practice in clinical midwifery care, *Information science and knowledge management*, 8: 73–92.

Morrison, T. (1996) Partnership and collaboration: rhetoric and reality, *Child Abuse and Neglect*, 20(2): 127–40.

Morrison, T. (2007) Emotional intelligence, emotion and social work: context, characteristics, complications and contribution. *British Journal of Social Work*, 37: 245–263.

Munro, E. (1996) Avoidable and unavoidable mistakes in child protection work, *British Journal of Social Work*, 26: 793–808.

Munro, E. (1999) *Common errors of reasoning in child protection work*, *Child Abuse and Neglect* 23(8): 745–58, available at LSE Research Articles Online: http://eprints.lse.ac.uk/358/

Munro, E. (2005) What tools do we need to improve identification of child abuse? *Child Abuse Review*, 14(6): 374–88.

Munro, E. (2008) *Effective child protection*, London: Sage.

Munro, E. (2011) *The Munro review of child protection: Final report: A child-centred system*, Cm 8062, May, London: Department for Education.

Murdock, G. (1997) Thin descriptions: questions of method in cultural analysis, in J. McGuigan (ed), *Cultural methodologies*, London: Sage, pp 178–92.

Neef, M.M. (2008) The forgotten map, *Resurgence*, No. 247, March/April.

Neet, D., Siesfeld, G.A. and Cefola, J. (1998) *The economic impact of knowledge*, Woburn: Butterworth-Heinemann.

Newcomb, T. (1953) An approach to the study of communication acts, *Psychological Review*, 60: 393–404.

Norman, D. (2004) *Emotion design: Why we love (or hate) everyday things*, Basic Books.

NSPCC (2015) Children in need: statistics 2013/14, available at: https://www.nspcc.org.uk/fighting-for-childhood/news-opinion/children-in-need-statistics/ (last accessed 4/12/15).

NSW Child Death Review Team (2000) *1998–99 Report. New South Wales Child Death Review Team*, NSW: Surrey Hills.

Ofsted (2005) *Safeguarding children: The second joint chief inspectors' report on the arrangements to safeguard children*, available at: www.safeguardingchildren.org.uk/Safeguarding-children/2005-report

Ofsted (2008) *Safeguarding children: The third joint chief inspectors' report on the arrangements to safeguard children*, available at: www. safeguardingchildren.org.uk/Safeguarding-children/2008-report

Osborne, S.P. (1998) *Voluntary organizations and innovation in public services*, London: Routledge.

Parton, N. (1985) *The politics of child abuse*, Basingstoke: Macmillian.

Parton, N. (1991) *Governing the family: Child care, child orotection and the state*, Basingstoke: Palgrave MacMillan.

Parton, N. (1996) Social work, risk and the 'blaming system', in N. Parton (ed), *Social theory, social change and social work*, London: Routledge.

Parton, N. (1997) *Child protection and family support: Tensions, contradictions, and possibilities*, London: Routledge.

Parton, N. (1998) Risk, advanced liberalism, and child welfare: the need to rediscover uncertainty and ambiguity, *British Journal of Social Work*, 28(1): 5–28.

Parton, N. (2006a) *Safeguarding childhood: Early intervention and surveillance in a late modern society*, Hampshire: Palgrave Macmillan.

Parton, N. (2006b) Every child matters: the shift to prevention whilst strengthening protection in children's services in England, *Children and Youth Services Review*, 28(8): 976–92.

Parton, N. (2008) Changes in the form of knowledge in social work: from the social to the informational, *British Journal of Social Work*, 38(2): 253–69.

Payne, L. (2004) Information sharing and assessment (ISA): can data management reduce risk? Policy review: *Children and Society*, 18: 383–86.

Payne, H. (2008) The jigsaw of child protection, *Journal of the Royal Society of Medicine*, 101(2): 93–94.

Pearce, W.B. (1989) *Communication and the human condition*, Carbondale, IL: Southern Illinois University Press.

Peckover, S., White, S. and Hall, C. (2008) Making and managing electronic children: e-assessment in child welfare, *Information, communication and society*, 11(3): 375–94.

Penna, S. (2005) The children act 2004: child protection and social surveillance, *Journal of Social Welfare and Family Law*, 27(2): 143–57.

Pettigrew, K.E. (1999) Waiting for chiropody: contextual results from an ethnographic study of the information behaviour among attendees at community clinics, *Information Processing and Management*, 35(6): 801–17.

Picard, R. (2000) *Affective computing*, Cambridge, MA: MIT University Press.

Pithouse, A. (1998) *Social work: The social organisation of an invisible trade*, Farnham: Ashgate.

Pithouse, A. and Broadhurst, K. (2009) The common assessment framework: effective innovation for children and young people with 'additional needs' or simply more technical hype?, in K. Broadhurst, C. Grover and J. Jamieson (eds), *Critical perspectives on safeguarding children*, Chichester: Wiley-Blackwell.

Platt, D. (2006) Threshold decisions: how social workers prioritise referrals of child concern, *Child Abuse Review*, 15(1): 4–18.

Pollner, M. (1987) *Mundane reason*, Cambridge: Cambridge University Press.

Pomerantz, A.M. (1986) Extreme case formulations: a new way of legitimating claims, *Human studies*, 9: 219–30.

Porter, H. (2010) The very civil Lib Dems, *Guardian*, 12 May, available at: http://www.theguardian.com/commentisfree/henryporter/2010/may/12/coalition-proposals-civil-rights

Potter, J. (1997) *Representing reality: Discourse, rhetoric and social construction*, London: Sage.

Reder, P. and Duncan, S. (2003) Understanding communication in child protection networks, *Child Abuse Review*, 12: 82–100.

Reder, P. and Duncan, S. (2004) Making the most of the Victoria Climbié inquiry report, *Child Abuse Review*, 13: 95–114.

Reder, P., Duncan, S. and Gray, M. (1993) *Beyond blame: Child abuse tragedies revisited*, London: Routledge.

Richardson, S. and Asthana, S. (2005) Policy and legal influences on inter-organisational information sharing in health and social care services, *Journal of Integrated Care*, 13(3): 3–10.

Richardson, S. and Asthana, S. (2006) Inter-agency information sharing in Health and Social Care Services: the role of professional culture, *British Journal of Social Work*, 36: 657–69.

Rorty, R. (1979) *Philosophy and the mirror of nature*, Princeton, NJ: Princeton University Press.

Sack, H. (1992) *Lectures on conversation*, Vols. I and II, ed. G. Jefferson, Oxford: Blackwell.

Sarangi, S. and Slembrouck, S. (1996) *Language, bureaucracy and social control*, London: Longman.

Schement, J.R. and Rubins, B. (1993) *Between communication and information* (Information behaviour, series 4), Colorado: Transaction Publishers.

Schon, D.A. (1983) *The reflexive professional*, New York, NY: Free Press.

Schon, D.A. (1991) *The reflective practitioner: How professionals think in action*, Aldershot: Avebury Academic Publishing.

Schutz, A. (1962) *Collected papers II: The problem of social reality*, The Hague: Martinus Nijhoff.

Schutz, A. and Luckmann, T. (1974) *The structures of the life-world*, London: Heinemann.

Seebohm, F. (1968) *Report of the committee on local authority and allied social services*, Cm 3703, London: HMSO.

Shaw, I., Bell, M., Sinclair, I., Sloper, P., Mitchell, W., Dyson, P., Clayden, J. and Rafferty, J. (2009) An exemplary scheme? An evaluation of the integrated children's system. *British Journal of Social Work*, 39: 613–26.

Sheppard, M. (1998) Practice validity, reflexivity and knowledge, *British Journal of Social Work*, 28(5): 763–81.

Siegel, D. (1999) *The developing mind: How relationships and the brain interact to shape who we are*, London: Guilford Press.

Sinclair, R. and Bullock, R. (2002) *Learning from past experience: A review of serious case reviews*, London: Department of Health.

Smith, D.E. (1990) *Texts, facts and femininity: Exploring the relations of ruling*, New York, NY: Routledge.

Social Work Task Force (2009) *Building a safe, confident future: The final report of the social work task force: November 2009*, London: DCSF.

Stevenson, L. (2015) Reflections of practice conversations, available at: CommunityCareonline (last accessed 02.09.15).

Steyaert, J. and Gould, N. (1999) Social services, social work and information management: some European perspectives, *European Journal of Social Work*, 2(2): 165–75.

Sundin, O. and Johannisson, J. (2005) The instrumentality of information needs and relevance. Information context: nature, impact and role. Lecture notes in *Computer Science*, vol 3507, 107-118.

Taylor, C. and White, S. (2000) *Practising reflexivity in health and welfare: making knowledge*, Buckingham: Open University Press.

Taylor, C. and White, S. (2001) Knowledge, truth and reflexivity: the problem of judgement in social work, *Journal of Social Work*, 1(1): 37–59.

Taylor, C. and White, S. (2006) Knowledge and reasoning in social work: educating humane judgement, *British Journal of Social Work*, 36(6): 937–54.

Tetlock, P.E. (2005) *Expert political judgment: How good is it? How can we know?* Princeton, NJ: Princeton University Press.

Teubner, G. (1983) Substantive and reflexive elements in modern law, *Law and Society Review*, 17(2): 239–85.

Tuominen, K. and Savolainen, R. (1997) A social constructionist approach to the study of information use as discursive action, in P. Vakkari, R. Savolainen and B. Devin (eds) *Information seeking in context: Proceeding of an international conference on research in information needs, seeking, and use in different contexts*, 14-16 August 1996, Tampere, Finland, London: Graham Taylor, pp 81-96.

Warren House Group Dartington Social Research Unit (2004) *Towards a common language for children in need*, Dartington: Dartington Social Research Unit.

Wastell, D.G. (2011) *Managers as designers in the public services: beyond techno-magic*, Axminster: Triarchy Press.

Wastell, D. and White, S. (2014) Making sense of complex electronic records: socio-technical design in social care, *Applied Ergonomics*, 45: 143:49.

Wastell, D., White, S., Broadhurst, K., Peckover, S. and Pithouse, A. (2010) Children's services in the iron cage of performance management: street level bureaucracy and the spectre of Švejkism, *International Journal of Social Work*, 19(3): 310–20.

Wattam, C. (1992) *Making a case in child protection*, Harlow: Longman.

Wattam, C. (1996) The social construction of child abuse for practical policy purposes – a review of child protection: messages from research, *Child and Family Law Quarterly*, 8(3): 189–200.

Wattam, C. (1997) Can filtering processes be rationalised? in N. Parton (ed) *Child protection and family support: Tensions, contradictions and possibilities*, London: Routledge, pp 109–25.

Weedon, C. (1997) *Feminist practices and poststructuralist theory*, (2nd edn), Oxford: Blackwell.

Wenger, E. (1998) *Communities of practice: Learning, meaning and identity*, New York, NY: Cambridge University Press.

Wetherell, M., Taylor, S. and Yates, S.J. (eds) (2001) *Discourse theory and practice: A reader*, London: Sage.

White, S. (2009) Arguing the case in safeguarding, in K. Broadhurst, C. Grover, and J. Jamieson (eds), *Critical perspectives on safeguarding children*, Chichester: Wiley-Blackwell, pp 93–110.

White, S. and Featherstone, B. (2005) Communicating misunderstandings: multi-agency work as social work practice, *Child and Family Social Work*, 10: 207–16.

White, S., Hall, C. and Peckover, S. (2009) The descriptive tyranny of the common assessment framework: technologies of categorization and professional practice in child welfare, *British Journal of Social Work*, 39: 1197–1217.

White, S., Wastell, D., Smith, S., Hall, C., Whitaker, E., Debelle, G., Mannion, R. and Waring, J. (2015) Improving practice in safeguarding at the interface between hospital services and children's social care: a mixed-methods case study, *Health Service Delivery Research*, 3(4): 1–194.

WHO (World Health Organisation) (2008) *Action on Patient Safety – High 5s*, available at: http://www.who.int/patientsafety/solutions/high5s/project_plan/en/

WHO (2009) *Human factors in patient safety review of topics and tools: Report for methods and measures working group of WHO patient safety*, available at: http://www.who.int/patientsafety/research/methods_measures/human_factors/human_factors_review.pdf

Williams, F. (2004) What matters is who works: why every child matters to New Labour: commentary on the DfES green paper *Every Child Matters*, *Critical Social Policy*, 24(3): 406–27.

Wilson, T.D. (1981) On user studies and information needs, *Journal of Documentation*, 37(1): 3–15.

Wilson, T.D. (1997) Information behaviour: an interdisciplinary perspective, *Information Processing and Management*, 33(4): 551–72.

Wilson, T.D. (1999) Models in information behaviour research, *Journal of Documentation*, 55(3): 249–70.

Wilson, T.D. (2006) Revisiting user studies and information needs, *Journal of Documentation*, 62(6): 680–84.

Wilson, T.D. and Brekke, N. (1996) Mental contamination and mental correction: unwanted influences on judgements and evaluations, *Psychological Bulletin*, 116(1): 117–42.

Wolfe D.A., Jaffe, P., Wilson, S.K. and Zak, L. (1985) Children of battered women: the relation of child behavior to family violence and maternal stress, *Journal of Consulting and Clinical Psychology*, 12: 39–41.

Index